For the students of Bailey's Elementary School for the Arts and Sciences. I have learned so much from you!

NUMBER SENSE ROUTINES

Building Numerical Literacy Every Day in Grades K–3

Jessica F. Shumway

Foreword by Lucy West

Stenhouse Publishers
Portland, Maine

Stenhouse Publishers
www.stenhouse.com

Credits
Page 57: Early Counting Learning Trajectory from *Learning and Teaching Early Math: The Learning Trajectories Approach* by Douglas H. Clements and Julie Sarama, published by Routledge, an imprint of Taylor & Francis Group. Copyright © 2009. Used with permission.

Library of Congress Cataloging-in-Publication Data
Shumway, Jessica F.
    Number sense routines : building numerical literacy every day in grades K–3 / Jessica F. Shumway.
        p. cm.—(Number sense routines)
    Includes bibliographical references and index.
    ISBN 978-1-57110-790-9 (pbk. : alk. paper)—ISBN 978-1-57110-901-9 (e-book)
    1. Mathematics—Study and teaching (Primary) 2. Mathematics—Study and teaching (Preschool) I. Title.
    QA135.53.S57 2011
    372.7'2—dc22

                                                                                2010045397

Cover, interior design, and typeset by Martha Drury

Manufactured in the United States of America
PRINTED ON 30% PCW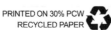
RECYCLED PAPER

17 16 15 14 13 12 11   9 8 7 6 5 4 3

CONTENTS

FOREWORD

by Lucy West

I love this book. *Number Sense Routines* belongs on the shelf of every elementary classroom teacher, beginning or experienced, who is willing to think deeply about how to develop his or her students' number sense.

Number sense is a catchall term frequently bandied about but rarely understood; it is often at the heart of the issues that plague American students who are struggling to learn mathematics and achieve high test scores. Unfortunately, number sense does not get developed deeply at the elementary grades, because the focus of the teaching is often on facts and skills. Anyone who truly understands mathematics understands that fluency with facts and skillful computation is the result of having number sense, not the other way around.

In this book, Jessica shows how easily number sense can be developed, no matter what curriculum materials teachers are using or what their standards or standardized tests require of them. Jessica takes familiar activities and gives them unprecedented depth, sophistication, and purpose. Her stellar work is an example of what excellence in teaching entails. She studies both her subject and her students deeply to develop her own understanding. She then works with colleagues to innovate and experiment until their collaborative efforts yield the desired results. Jessica's respectful engagement with her students and colleagues is contagious. She invites everyone to dive deeply into the learning process and face the often overwhelming and sometimes misguided demands of our time. Instead of becoming compliant, Jessica becomes curious, playful, and creative. How refreshing!

Jessica takes the reader on a practical journey through the intricacies of using routines to meet the needs of a wide range of students. What's more, she makes it seem doable—even easy. She shows how these seemingly simple routines provide a wealth of informal assessment data. She explains specifically what to look for and how to analyze student work from a positive perspective rather than a deficit model. We see how she responds to the work in differentiated and specific ways to assist individual students in their development.

Jessica's impressive understanding of how to assess and guide students' capacity to think, reason, and deepen their understanding of important mathematical ideas becomes accessible to the reader. She demonstrates how using ten to fifteen minutes of focused time on routines, on a regular basis, results in remarkable resiliency and engagement from the students. She shows us how to "play" with simple routines to go beyond memorization and drill to develop deep understanding, fluency, flexibility, accuracy, and elegance in student thinking and capacity to compute. She uses actual classroom excerpts to help the reader learn to make student thinking visible through simple yet profound talking and listening routines, sentence frames, and teacher questions.

Jessica speaks so clearly and with such love for teaching and children. This book reminded me that teaching is both an art and a science, and that true educators go beyond mandates and test scores to do what is best for students. Jessica is an exemplary learner, teacher, and coach. She is both scientific in her approach to teaching and learning and artful in her interactions with students and colleagues. She is the quintessential educator as she seeks out professional learning opportunities that inform her practice and then takes what she learns, applies it, and develops it further.

Jessica shows the reader specifically how to construct, sequence, and implement counting activities, calendar routines, computational routines, and so forth. She names the characteristics of high-leverage, high-yield routines, explaining that they must allow access to all students and that they should be built around important mathematical concepts such as place value, equivalence, the search for pattern and relationships, and so on. In so doing, she demonstrates how all students, even struggling learners and those who need to be challenged, can learn with and from one another in the same activity.

Her descriptions of and directions for each of the activities are easy to follow, thorough, nuanced, and designed to assist teachers to easily incorporate these routines into their practice and to implement them with intelligence. She shows the reader step-by-step what to focus on, how to get students to reveal their thinking, and what questions to ask. She empowers the reader to innovate and learn to teach important mathematics—not just skills and facts.

Jessica does what so many educators need to learn to do. She mindfully engages with curriculum materials, studies her children closely, and then experiments with activities and interventions until she gets results. She sets up—and shares with the reader—tools she has developed to keep track of her work and what students are learning. She tweaks and tinkers and adjusts what appear to be simple activities into carefully crafted routines worth doing over and over again, because they bring out the brilliance in her students, improve their understanding, and increase test scores.

Jessica scaffolds each activity for the teacher. She takes complex ideas like number sense and place value and unpacks them with simple examples and clear definitions. She puts ideas in the context of student learning, as well as student and teacher interactions, and brings them alive in ways that make them accessible to educators of all levels of mathematics understanding. Her explanation of the big ideas in each activity is coupled with how they relate to student levels of understanding. She shows the reader how to make adjustments to these routines to increase or decrease the cognitive demand for individuals or groups of students. She describes—through mini-cases and classroom vignettes—student learning at different levels and then gives the reader specific variations of each routine to address the needs of students at all stages of understanding. And she has included a wealth of tools, references, and recording sheets that make the job of teaching in the twenty-first century not only manageable but also effective and responsive.

I am proud to say that I know and have worked with Jessica. She is a remarkable educator, a skillful coach, and a strong new voice in the field. I imagine *Number Sense Routines* will become one of those dog-eared books that educators will keep on their desks for frequent guidance, and I look forward to reading her future books. Thank you, Jessica, for this wonderful contribution.

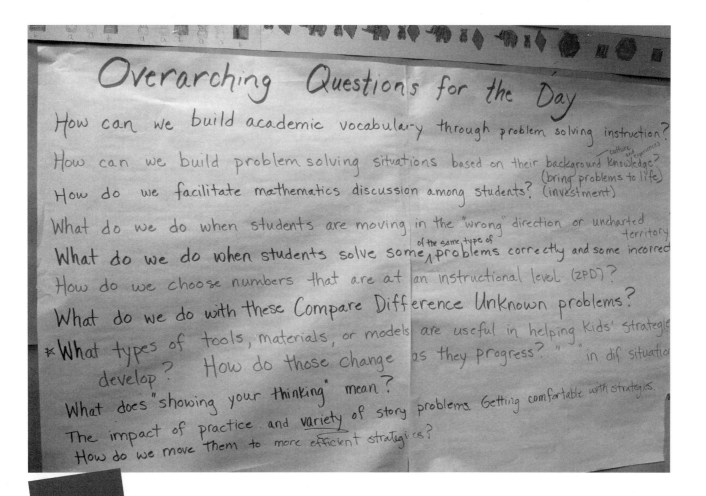

Overarching Questions for the Day

How can we build academic vocabulary through problem solving instruction?

How can we build problem solving situations based on their background knowledge? (culture and experiences)

How do we facilitate mathematics discussion among students? (bring problems to life) (investment)

What do we do when students are moving in the "wrong" direction or uncharted territory

What do we do when students solve some of the same type of problems correctly and some incorrect

How do we choose numbers that are at an instructional level (ZPD)?

What do we do with these Compare Difference Unknown problems?

* What types of tools, materials, or models are useful in helping kids' strategies develop? How do those change as they progress? " " in dif situation

What does "showing your thinking" mean?

The impact of practice and variety of story problems. Getting comfortable with strategies.

How do we move them to more efficient strategies?

ACKNOWLEDGMENTS

T he collection of questions in the photograph above comes from a group of highly dedicated teachers at Bailey's Elementary School for the Arts and Sciences—teachers with whom I had the privilege of working during the 2007–2008 school year. My colleague Mimi Granados and I started a professional learning cohort at our school and called it the Math Collaborative. Math Collaborative was designed to provide teachers with a mathematics teaching course combined with one-on-one coaching. The goals of Math Collaborative were to develop robust pedagogical math content knowledge and expand each teacher's toolbox of instructional strategies. We led this yearlong professional study group and coached prekindergarten through fifth-grade teachers in their mathematics class-rooms. As evident from the questions in the photo, numeracy was at the core of our discussions and struggles. These teachers pushed my thinking and one another's thinking as we worked through math content, discussed instructional philosophies and strategies, and investigated students' thinking and understandings at a deep level. These teachers were willing to think critically and challenge their beliefs about their teaching and children's mathematical learning.

The 2007–2008 Math Collaborative
Back row, left to right:
Mimi Granados, Amy Henrickson, Rosalba Mendoza, Elena Duarte, Vivian Greblo, Karen McCarthy, Albert Chong, Kassia Wedekind, and Maria Tincoff.
Front row, left to right:
Mary Anne Buckley, Ada Prabhavat, Carol Velez, Stanzi Lowe, and Jessica Shumway.

We realized that mathematics is messy. Our questions and concerns were not going to be answered quickly or easily. There's not one way to learn or teach mathematics. But the key to students' success in mathematics is being responsive to students' knowledge and understandings and building instruction from what students can do. I wrote this book to honor these teachers, who were so willing to ask questions, question each other, debate ideas, and open up their teaching and their students' learning to the group. I learned so much from them and their students about children's mathematical understandings, thinking, and learning. Thank you, Math Collaborative, Year 1!

The number sense routines discussed in this book come out of my own teaching, from the math teachers I worked with at Bailey's Elementary in Virginia, and from my work with Lucy West, Gwenanne Salkind, and the Title I math teachers in Fairfax County Public Schools. I rely on a variety of resources. Please take note of the references for further reading and resources.

In addition, I have been inspired by researchers and practitioners throughout my career. I draw knowledge from many, including the researchers of Cognitively Guided Instruction (Thomas Carpenter, Elizabeth Fennema, Linda Levi, Megan Franke, Susan Empson, and Linda Jaslow), the writers and curriculum developers of the *Developing Mathematical Ideas* and the *Investigations* curricula (including Susan Jo Russell, Deborah Schifter, Virginia Bastable, and Karen Economopoulos), and the educators involved in the Mathematics in the City project (including Catherine Fosnot and Maarten Dolk). I also have been influenced by the work of numerous authors, including Lucy West, Douglas Clements, Juanita Copley, Kathy Richardson, Marilyn Burns, John Van de Walle, Lauren Resnick, Karen Fuson, Suzanne Chapin, James Hiebert, and Constance Kamii, among others. In addition, my mathematics coach and mentor, Debbie Gates, has provided me with numerous readings and research to learn from and reflect on. She's a wealth of resources and has guided my learning throughout the years. I have been very fortunate to work in a county, and in schools, that place a high value on professional development. To Gwenanne Salkind and Jay McClain, thank you for the many and varied professional development opportunities you encouraged me to be involved in.

I have been fortunate to spend time with many teachers and their students in their classrooms. I wish to extend my gratitude to Mary Anne Buckley, Carrie Cantillana, Michelle Gale, Amy Henrickson, Christy Hermann, Emelie Parker, and Kassia Wedekind. Thank you for allowing me to write about our experiences in your classrooms. I love investigating teaching and learning with you! I also want to thank Mary Anne Buckley, Amy Henrickson, Matt Lintner, and Emelie Parker for reading early drafts of various parts of the manuscript and providing feedback and encouragement.

To Suzanne Whaley, thank you for your reading of many chapters, for your ability to read my mind and know what I'm trying to say, and for our discussions about numeracy and literacy over the years. You were instrumental in helping me tighten my writing, see various perspectives, and make connections among themes, ideas, and topics.

Mimi Granados, thank you for helping me gather last-minute pieces I needed—you have always been "the details person," catching the details I overlook because I'm lost in the big picture. In addition, thank you for embarking on many math adventures with me.

Many thanks go to Kathleen Fay for getting me started on writing a book. Without the bug you put in my ear, I don't know if I would have even imagined this book-writing journey.

I am grateful for the incredible team at Stenhouse Publishers. Thank you to Chris Downey, Rebecca Eaton, Jay Kilburn, and Dan Tobin. Erin Trainer, I appreciate your sharp eye, amazing attention to detail, and patience with my many, many drawings and boxes of information. I also want to thank an anonymous outside reader for her multiple readings of the manuscript. Her knowledge and experience guided me to reflect, revise, and re-revise, which greatly improved the final product.

I have a very special thank you to Toby Gordon, my editor at Stenhouse Publishers. Toby, thank you for believing in me and in the teaching and learning ideas I wanted to share with teachers. I am extraordinarily grateful for your persistence, flexibility, patience, gentle nudges, knowledge, talent, and last, but not least, unwavering support and encouragement throughout the project. Furthermore, it is a pleasure and a privilege to be part of a forum of teachers who write for teachers, which you and Stenhouse provide for us.

These professional books allow us to have ongoing conversations about teaching and learning with one another all across the world.

Finally, I want to let my students and their families know how much I appreciate them. Families, I will always treasure our Family Fridays full of doughnuts, math fun, drama, and poetry. Students, thank you for allowing me to share your conversations, thinking, and learning with other teachers and students. I enjoy learning how your brains all think differently, appreciate how you all support and care for each other, and am grateful for our many days of teaching each other and learning from one another.

INTRODUCTION

Kevin is still counting by ones on the number grid and I am not sure how to help him move to a more efficient strategy.

—Second-grade teacher

Maria is in third grade and still uses her fingers for simple facts like 8 + 8. She should know that fact, or at least have a more efficient strategy by now. What do I do?

—Third-grade teacher

These are typical concerns I heard from teachers during my years as a mathematics coach. When children have large gaps in their number sense, teachers get stuck: Why do some students struggle with developing their number sense? How much time do we give students to develop particular strategies and understandings? When do we intervene? Teachers see that students lacking

1

number sense fall further and further behind their peers in all areas of mathematics. What can teachers do to overcome these hurdles? Of equal or greater importance, how do we help students develop strong number sense right from the beginning?

This book is about tapping into every child's innate sense of number, providing daily experiences to develop and nourish number sense, and facilitating students' application of number sense in a variety of situations and contexts. Doing these things can, at times, seem daunting. The aim of this book is to equip you with a toolbox for providing students with number sense experiences through the use of number sense routines every day.

The routines serve as "warm-ups"—quick five-minute, ten-minute, or fifteen-minute number sense experiences at the beginning of your math class. Children need these kinds of *daily* experiences with number sense as well as a variety of opportunities to apply number sense concepts. The "daily-ness"—the everyday interactions—with numbers, amounts, patterns, and relationships will build your students' number sense.

The journey of number sense will be continuous and ongoing for your students. It's fascinating to observe their different learning paths as they acquire number sense understandings. As you read, you will step into various classrooms and listen in on students' conversations, which I hope will give you insight into the power of number sense routines and the impact they have on students' number sense development. My hope is that by going into the classroom, into students' conversations, and into their thought processes, you will come away with new ideas and tools to use in your own classroom. The classroom examples, combined with various resources, such as photos, "What's the Math?" boxes, and boxes of questions for differentiation, demonstrate how students' number sense develops over time and will help you be more keenly aware of what mathematics concepts and strategies to look for in your students' discussions and work. The more you know what to look for, the easier it becomes to facilitate students' learning and help them deepen their number sense.

I learn the most when I really listen to students and find out where they are in their individual learning paths. I reflect on what number sense experiences will move them further along in their number sense journey. That journey is different for everyone.

PART I

BUILDING NUMBER SENSE THROUGH ROUTINES

1

NUMBER SENSE

What Does It Mean?

During an autumn morning in our third-grade classroom, four students and I were problem solving at the circular table in the back of the classroom while the rest of the students worked in their math stations. The four students were working diligently to unravel the following problem:

> 600 monarch butterflies were overwintering in an oyamel tree in Mexico.
> One spring day, 378 of them flew away.
> How many are still in the oyamel tree?

I used this problem as an informal preassessment, purposely choosing these numbers and this problem type in order to learn more about my students' number sense and mathematical reasoning. I was expecting a range of ideas and strategies and wanted to see what these four students would do with the problem. After they worked independently for several minutes, sure enough, a math debate over the solution surfaced.

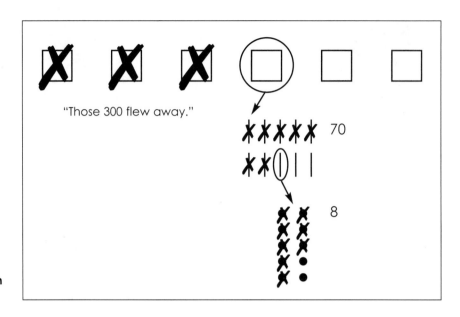

"Those 300 flew away."

Figure 1.1
Brandon's Strategy Using a Base Ten Block Representation

"I know we have to subtract, because the butterflies flew away, but it's not possible," said Carlos. "You can't do 600 minus 378 because of the zeros. You can't do 0 minus 8 or 0 minus 7."

"Yes, you can. Look what I did," said Sumayah. "Six hundred minus 378 is 378. See? Look."

"Wait, what did you do?" asked Anita.

Sumayah attempted to prove that her strategy worked: "I did 0 minus 8 is 8, 0 minus 7 is 7, and 6 minus 3 is 3."

Anita, still confused by Sumayah's answer and strategy, said, "I don't get it . . . I don't know if that works. I got a different answer. I got 222."

While these three students were talking, Brandon was still working on the problem. He drew six flats to represent 600 butterflies, crossed out three of the flats to show that he took away 300 (those that flew away), and was now working on taking out 78 from one of the hundreds that was left (see Figure 1.1).

There was a lot going on in this group of four third-grade mathematicians. Carlos was thinking about the standard algorithm for 600 – 378, but the regrouping procedure stopped him from solving the problem. He would have had no problem if it had been 678 – 300. But with 600 – 378, he didn't know where to start, because he believed he couldn't subtract 8 from 0 or 7 from 0.

Sumayah, who was also focusing on the standard algorithm, changed the problem to 678 – 300. She didn't see that she had actually changed the whole problem in an effort to solve it.

Brandon was using number sense to solve the problem, although his strategy was not yet efficient. By drawing base ten blocks, he was able to visualize the problem and the amounts. The six flats helped him see the amount

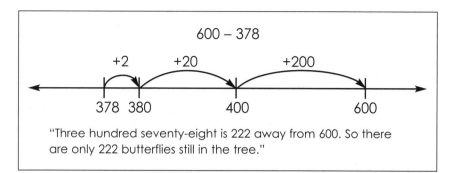

$600 - 378$

"Three hundred seventy-eight is 222 away from 600. So there are only 222 butterflies still in the tree."

Figure 1.2
Anita's Solution

of 600. He immediately took out 300 because those 300 butterflies flew away. Then, he looked at what was left (300 butterflies) and was figuring out how to take 78 out of one of the hundreds. While Brandon was working that out, Anita launched into why 222 was the correct solution.

"How did you get that?" I asked, trying to understand her thinking.

"I wrote down 600 minus 378. I know that the number of butterflies still in the tree will be less than 300 because half of 600 is 300 and we are taking more than 300 out of 600. It will be 200-something. I sort of did it in my head. If I add 2 to 78, that takes me to 80. It's easier to count by tens. Then I counted up 20 to get to 400. Then, from 400 it is 200 away to 600, so altogether, 378 is 222 away from 600. So there are only 222 butterflies still in the tree." (See Figure 1.2 for a representation of Anita's thinking.)

Before Anita even began working out the problem, she looked at the numbers and thought about the relationship between them. "I know that the number of butterflies still in the tree will be less than 300 because half of 600 is 300." She was thinking about 600 as an amount and 378 as an amount, then recognized that there is a doubling/halving relationship between 600 and 300. Also embedded in Anita's explanation was the relationship between subtraction and addition, another big idea with which students need to grapple. She understood that she could use addition in this problem because she was finding the difference between two numbers. Also, Anita's sense of place value is strong. She was easily able to think about 378 as an amount made up of 300, 70, and 8, and used each place in the number to get to friendly numbers (like tens and hundreds). Although Anita didn't use the term *number line*, she was most likely thinking about the numbers in a number line model and mentally making jumps on it. She acknowledged, "I sort of did it in my head."

Anita is an example of a student with strong number sense. Brandon is on his way. He's working on solidifying his visual understandings of number. Sumayah and Carlos did not exhibit number sense in their strategies. In this discussion they were not thinking about 600 and 378 as amounts. They were only thinking about a procedure and trying to recall the steps to take.

As teachers, having a strong understanding of what number sense is and of all of its components and complexities will improve our abilities to plan experiences that will develop and nurture our students' number sense. Our knowledge and understanding of number sense will help us know what to look for as our students work through problems and travel along the path to a robust sense of number.

WHY FOCUS ON NUMBER SENSE?

Students who struggle in math often lack number sense. It is difficult to compute without number sense. It is a struggle to find relationships among numbers or equations without number sense. It is more arduous to figure out measurement, geometry, and data problems without number sense. In other words, number sense is the foundational building block for all strands of mathematics.

As students build their number sense, mathematics takes on greater meaning. Mathematics becomes more about reaching understandings than following rigid sets of rules. With strong number sense, children become more apt to attempt problems and make sense of mathematics. It is the key to understanding all math.

WHAT IS NUMBER SENSE?

So, what is number sense, exactly? Think of a student who has strong number sense, someone like Anita. Anita understands numbers, ways to represent numbers, relationships among numbers, and number systems. She makes reasonable estimates, computes fluently, uses reasoning strategies (e.g., relates operations, like addition and subtraction, to one another), and uses visual models (e.g., a mental number line) based on her number sense to figure out a problem.

Number sense is complex. (See Box 1.1 for more about number sense.) There are many layers to it, and it is rooted within all strands of mathematics. Number sense facilitates problem solving, reasoning, and discussing mathematical ideas. One way to *begin* to unpack the term *number sense* is to think of students who, like Anita, are on the path to developing a strong sense of number. These students typically demonstrate these understandings and skills:

- A sense of what numbers mean. For example, they can visualize in their heads how much 100 is or can "see" what $\frac{1}{4}$ looks like (such as one slice of a pie cut into fourths). Someone with a sense of what numbers mean has a visual model and concrete understanding of quantities.
- An ability to look at the world in terms of quantity and numbers. For example, they understand the relative magnitude of an amount, such as when 100 is a lot and when it's not much at all. A hundred people in a room is a lot, whereas 100 grains of sand is not much sand at all. Students

WHAT'S THE MATH?
Early Number Sense Learning Trajectory

Douglas Clements (2007, 2008) explains young learners' number sense development in terms of a learning trajectory. Catherine Fosnot and Maarten Dolk (2001a, 2001b, 2002) describe big ideas and strategies within a landscape of learning. The more we as teachers know about these big ideas in students' mathematical development, the better we are able to support students' numerical literacy by planning appropriate routines for their mathematical development.

Subitizing: Humans (and scientists believe the same is true for some animals) are able to see small amounts (usually five or fewer) as a whole and can perceive the amount without counting. One of my kindergarten students, Layla, could show me immediately and accurately "how many" on her fingers long before she was able to count. I would put out four cubes and she would immediately show me four fingers, although she could not tell me how many. This is *perceptual subitizing*—she could perceive four without counting. *Conceptual subitizing* occurs when students perceptually subitize two or more amounts, then combine the amounts automatically (Clements 1999). For example, a student might recognize six objects immediately because she saw three and three and knew that when combined, that makes six.

Magnitude: Before children know how to count, they are able to tell you which of two sets has more without counting. Their sense of magnitude is apparent early on.

Counting: There are also learning trajectories for counting, according to Clements (2007, 2008). Children are able to say the counting sequence before their one-to-one correspondence is fully developed.

One-to-one correspondence: Students with one-to-one correspondence say one number for each object counted.

Cardinality: When you count a group of objects, the last number you say tells how many there are in all. Students who do not yet have cardinality recount the objects when asked, "How many?"

Hierarchical inclusion: Numbers build by exactly one each time—smaller numbers are part of bigger numbers. Children who have constructed the idea of hierarchical inclusion know that if you have six rocks and you take one away, there are five, or if you add a rock, there are seven. It's the idea of one more and one less.

Part/whole relationships: Once children begin to understand hierarchical inclusion, they begin to consider parts of a number. For example, they understand that 6 is made up of 5 and 1, 4 and 2, and 3 and 3.

Compensation: Children begin to see the parts of the whole and then are able to compensate. For example, if 5 plus 1 equals 6, then I also know that 4 plus 2 equals 6, because 4 is one less than 5, and 2 is one more than 1. One was removed from 5 and was given to the 2 in order to get the same amount.

Unitizing: As children gain a solid understanding of the preceding early number sense ideas, the idea of *unitizing* is constructed as they work with larger numbers (Fosnot and Dolk 2001a, 2001b). Twenty is made up of nineteen and one, eighteen and two, and so on. Twenty is also made up of two tens—students make this leap in understanding that they are now using "two" to represent two groups of something, in this case two groups of ten. The numeral *2* takes on different meanings depending on where it is in the number. That's a big idea in mathematics and a difficult understanding to construct!

For further explanation about early number sense, see *Young Mathematicians at Work: Constructing Number Sense, Addition, and Subtraction* by Catherine Twomey Fosnot and Maarten Dolk (2001a) as well as the articles and work of Douglas Clements (1999, 2007, 2008; Sarama and Clements 2009) of the University of Buffalo.

use this knowledge to make comparisons, interpret data, estimate, and answer the question, *Does that answer make sense in this situation/problem?*

- An ability to make comparisons among quantities. For example, they know that 300 is 400 away from 700 by using a mental number line, or know that there is a bigger difference between 50 and 150 than between 1,000 and 1,050. Students with strong number sense make comparisons using their sense of the quantities, using landmark numbers such as 10, 50, and 100, and using a mental number line (understanding where numbers fall along a number line).

- Flexibility, automaticity, and fluidity with numbers. For example, these students are able to solve problems quickly and efficiently because they use the five- and ten-structures of numbers (*7 is made up of a 5 and 2*), place-value understandings (*152 is made up of 100 and 50 and 2*), and relationships among numbers (*48 + 52 = 100 because I know 50 + 50 = 100 . . . I took 2 from the 52 and gave it to the 48 to make two 50s, because 50 is an easier number to work with*). Students with strong number sense apply their understanding of number systems to solve problems as well as reason through number relationships.

- An ability to perform mental math. For example, they are able to solve 20 + 35 in their heads by breaking apart numbers into tens and ones (*20 + 35 = 20 + 30 + 5*) or by counting up by tens (*20 + 35 = 55 because I can count on from 35 with two jumps of tens: 45, 55*). Students who can perform mental math often use what they know to solve other problems, for example, using knowledge of 7 + 7 to solve 7 + 8 (*7 + 8 = 7 + 7 + 1*).

- Flexibility with problems. For example, these students are able to show or tell two ways to solve a problem, or they are able to understand multiple ways to approach a problem.

- Automatic use of math information. For example, they are able to readily use what they know about numbers and number relationships to solve a problem and/or are able to draw on knowledge and strategies used in the past to solve new problems.

- An ability to determine reasonableness of an answer. For example, Anita knew that her answer to 600 − 378 would be less than 300, because half of 600 is 300 and she was taking away more than half.

- An ability to decide on a strategy based on the numbers in a problem (Fosnot and Dolk 2001a). For example, students with number sense will not use the algorithm to solve 100 − 95, because that is inefficient. Rather, they know that 95 is only 5 away from 100. They might, however, employ the algorithm for a problem like 127,582 − 34,391. There is no single strategy that is best for all problems. A strategy is more efficient and makes more sense based on the numbers, the situation, and the problem. Someone with number sense looks at the numbers first to decide on a strategy.

Embedded in these characteristics of number sense are big mathematical ideas; strategies that utilize number sense; skills, models, and tools for using number sense; and language for explaining number sense ideas and strategies (see Figure 1.3). As you read about number sense routines in Part II, look for the boxes titled "What's the Math?" This is where I highlight the various components of number sense within the context of a routine.

Although number sense is quite complex and has many components, thinking of students like Anita gives us a *sense* of number sense. Anita has a good start and has a lot of the essential components of number sense.

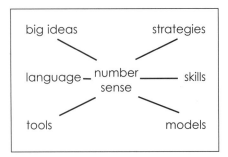

Figure 1.3
Components of Number Sense

However, she is nowhere near done. It is a journey, and she will continuously build her number sense as she acquires new understanding about multiplication and division, fractions and decimals, measurement, algebra, and so on. Building number sense is a process, and each of your students is in a different place within that process. Nevertheless, the goal for students is to build understanding and become numerically literate, that is, apply their number sense and know when to use which skills or strategies.

TEACHING FOR NUMBER SENSE: A PROCESS LEADING TO UNDERSTANDING

Before children even come to school, their intuitive sense of number begins to develop. They are able to recognize amounts of one, two, and three without counting (Sarama and Clements 2009). They develop a sense of more and less. Early on, young children come into contact with a variety of situations that involve quantities, and they begin to experience relationships among quantities and to problem solve. When a three-year-old says, "He has more," he is comparing amounts without counting and is understanding the magnitude of each group (Fosnot and Dolk 2001a, 35). By the time they come to school, children already have a store of informal math knowledge (Carpenter et al. 1999).

Teaching for number sense involves students building understandings from within and taking an active part in constructing their number sense. Part of this is knowing that there are multiple ways of approaching a problem and that they are capable of reasoning, finding relationships, and solving problems. I think Lauren Resnick said it best when she stated, "Only if children come to believe that there are always multiple ways to solve problems, and that they, personally, are capable of discovering some of these ways, will they be likely to exercise—and thereby develop—number sense" (1990). The numerically literate student trusts her strategies and application of number sense. The student sees herself as someone who can make sense of situations involving numbers and knows that there are a variety of ways to arrive at a solution.

In order to get to that point, a student needs multiple opportunities to bump into number sense ideas, use number sense, and discuss number sense ideas and strategies with peers. This is where we come in! We are there to set up number sense experiences, facilitate discussions, and support students' understandings as they journey toward numerical literacy. I believe students need to benefit from these number sense experiences *every day*. Daily routines are one way to ensure that students have a plethora of opportunities to further develop their number sense.

2

IMPROVING NUMBER SENSE

Routines That Are Not Routinized

A routine is an activity or event that occurs on a regular basis over a period of time. Think about the routines you already have in your classroom—greeting students in the morning, backpack procedures, morning meeting rituals, taking attendance, lunch count and lunch line procedures, read-alouds, calendar routines, weather observations and graphs, and author's share, just to name a few. Routines provide frameworks for our day. Our routines build community and create a safe learning environment for students. Routines provide feelings of belonging, ownership, and predictability, which make the classroom a place to take risks, try new things, and be successful.

Routines are a regular part of most math workshops and math lessons. You find them in curriculum materials, such as the math message in *Everyday Mathematics* (University of Chicago School Mathematics Project 2007) and ten-minute math in *Investigations in Number, Data, and Space* (TERC 2008). Many teachers begin their math block with some kind of warm-up. My purpose is to help you take what you are already doing with math routines and refine it to expand students' number sense. In this book I show you how to go beyond the curriculum materials to design routines based on your students' unique strengths and needs. These number sense routines are not "auto pilot" activities, but opportunities for meaningful practice. You'll learn when to use a particular routine, how to differentiate, and how to use routines as formative assessment tools. We'll also explore the mathematics behind the routines and take a look at paths students take as they develop their number sense.

A ROUTINE IN ACTION: COUNT AROUND THE CIRCLE

I shook the rain stick, our signal to clean up from quiet time and transition into math workshop. My fourth-grade students put their materials away and made their way over to the community circle. As Jose plopped down beside me, he asked, "Are we counting by hundreds today?" I gave him the heads up that we would be counting backward by tens. He began counting backward from ninety by tens quietly to himself as his classmates got settled.

Within two minutes everyone was ready. They were sitting in a circle on the floor and were ready to "count around the circle." I began our routine by saying, "Let's start with 188 and count backward by tens around the circle. If I start with 188 and we move clockwise around the circle, what do you think Catie will land on?" Catie was sitting directly across from me, about halfway around our circle of twenty-two students.

Anthony estimated, "Somewhere in the hundreds, like close to 118 or 108, because we'll go pretty far down the number line if we are counting by tens."

Marjorie said, "Maybe close to Anthony's guess, but maybe a little less than 100."

Nisaa added on to Marjorie's idea and said, "I agree with Marjorie, because Catie's about the tenth person and we're counting by tens. That means that it will be about 100 less than 188 . . . so, around 88?"

We had a quick discussion reinforcing the idea that an estimate does not have to be exact by looking at words that Anthony, Marjorie, and Nisaa used: *somewhere, close, about, around,* and *maybe.* We briefly talked about why numbers like 178 and 268 would not be good estimates. The number 178 is only one jump of ten away from 188—that estimate did not make sense because the first person to count would say that number. The number 268 is more than 188—this wouldn't make sense because we said we would be counting backward, not forward.

I started the count for that day's sequence by saying, "Let's try it . . . 188."

Jose, the first person, said, "One hundred seventy-eight," and then we continued around the circle. I wrote each number on an open number line as someone said it (see Figure 2.1). The visual scaffold was helpful for the majority of the class, although in different ways. It helped the few students who were still struggling with this skill of counting backward by tens, as it allowed them

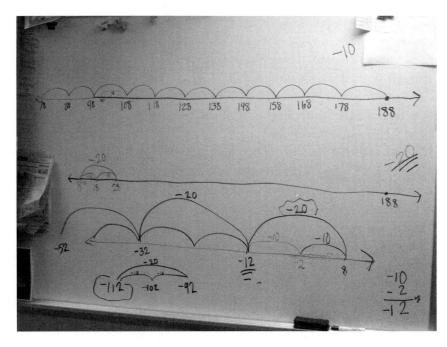

Figure 2.1

to participate in the counting activity. The majority of the students, however, did not need the visual scaffold to support their skill of counting backward by tens. But it helped these students to really understand the pattern and later apply it to other situations, for example, counting backward by twenty.

We continued to count smoothly around the circle, each person saying a number aloud while everyone else counted in their heads: "One hundred sixty-eight, 158, 148 . . ." Then, Adam got stuck. Adib, the person before him, said, "One hundred eight." Everyone waited silently, knowing that Adam would figure it out. He looked at Anthony and restated "One hundred twenty-eight," then looked at Melanie and restated "118," then restated Adib's number, "108." He said, "One hundred?" I wrote *100* on the number line, showing that it was 8 away from 108. That visual scaffold on the open number line was just enough support, and he said, "Ninety-eight!" Adam was one of the students still working to keep the visual number line model in his head. He wasn't quite fluent and automatic yet; nevertheless, he was able to solve the problem.

When we got to Catie, she said, "Seventy-eight," and we all nodded, confirming our estimates. I stopped them when we got to 8 in order to revisit the estimates and talk about Adam's strategy for figuring out the jump to 98.

Then, we tried counting backward by twenty, this time all the way around the circle. I again drew the open number line, but did not write each number as the students counted. I encouraged them to "see the jumps" in their heads as we counted around the circle. When Antonio got stuck, I drew a support on the number line to scaffold his strategy for figuring out what would come next (see Figure 2.1). We held a brief discussion about how the pattern changed after zero (8, –12, –32, . . .), how the tens place was no longer even but now odd, and that we were "adding even though we [were] subtracting." They were very excited to see this change of events. I asked them to keep thinking about these numbers, the patterns, and why this change happened. I assured them that we'd have more opportunities to look at these interesting negative numbers. They knew they needed to keep thinking about the "why," and we then moved on to the multiplication mini-lesson I'd planned for that day.

This Count Around the Circle routine, which is discussed in depth in Chapter 4, is a typical start to our math workshop. The predictability and ritualistic nature of routines in our classroom helps everyone feel at ease and participate, which promotes successful learning. Every day after our ten minutes of quiet time—which is our independent choice or rest time after lunch and recess to help us refocus for the afternoon—we come to the rug and sit in a circle. When I say, "Today we will Count Around the Circle," or "Today we will play with quantities on the ten-frames" (discussed in Chapter 3), students know what that particular ritual entails. We know what to do. We know what to expect. It's a comfortable and successful start to our math workshop each day.

In addition, the daily routine time gets students actively involved as they review number sense concepts and play with new number sense ideas; it also allows teachers time for formative assessment. In our case on that day, students had an opportunity to practice their estimation skills, practice counting backward by tens and twenties, continue to notice patterns in place value when counting, and begin exploring new ideas about negative numbers.

Number sense routines are a form of practice, but they are deep, meaningful practice. They serve to reteach, reinforce, and enrich. They maximize our time with students because they allow us to give our students multiple opportunities to strengthen and develop number sense. I find that number sense routines work most effectively when they occur at the same time each day. The predictable structure helps students make connections among routines from one day to the next. For example, in my fourth-grade classroom, we discussed the reasonableness of estimates before counting around the circle, because in the days prior, students' estimates were often way off or they were trying to calculate rather than estimate. Sometimes their estimates didn't fit with an obvious pattern. For instance, some students were making odd number estimates for a counting sequence that involved counting by twos starting at an even number.

In the days that followed this counting example, students started figuring out that Nisaa's estimates were frequently *really* close to the actual answer (without calculating it exactly). They started paying more attention to her estimation strategies and tried to figure out why her estimates were reasonable and so close to the exact answer without calculation. With the repeated experiences, my students made connections from one day to the next and were really figuring out what it means to estimate. As they made those day-to-day connections about estimation, they were also practicing a variety of counting sequences each day we did the routine. This practice over time helped my students gain understandings of relationships among numbers on the number line and notice patterns in place value. The children applied these understandings to their computation strategies and skills. The fluency with counting and the understanding of place value helped them become better and more efficient problem solvers. Lastly, the counting sequence in this example led the children to explore new ideas about negative numbers. The benefits of the counting routine during those weeks were deep, meaningful, and varied.

The number sense routines explored in this book are "responsive" routines—they are responsive to students' discussions, understandings, and learning needs. All of the routines in this book do the following:

- Provide daily number sense experiences
- Include discussion about numbers and their relationships
- Respond to students' current understandings
- Build on students' existing number sense
- Encourage students to play with numbers and enrich their mathematical thinking
- Help students make connections to big ideas in mathematics

In other words, number sense routines provide a daily framework for number sense practice, yet these routines are responsive to students. They are fluid and flexible. In *The Morning Meeting Book*, Roxann Kriete and Lynn Bechtel say, "There is a sensitive balance between the lovely sense of security that routine can provide and the monotony that can creep in when that routine is unlivened and unleavened" (2002, 29). Routines provide a comfortable predictability, but at the same time, we plan routines that will keep students challenged, provide opportunities to practice using their number sense, and reteach when necessary.

WHY FOCUS ON ROUTINES?

If your classroom is similar to the average classroom nationwide, chances are that the range of learners is wide, from the student struggling with number sense to the student who continually needs a challenge. More and more teachers are using a math workshop format to meet the diverse needs of their students. There are many ways to set up a math workshop. Some teachers structure them as follows:

- Warm-up (or math message or ten-minute math)
- Mini-lesson

- Guided math groups
  The teacher meets with small groups of four to five students while other students work in math stations, work on projects, problem solve, or work on a math game.
- Reflection or share

Other teachers set up their math workshops like this:

- Warm-up
- Mini-lesson
- Active learning or guided practice
  Students work on an activity or some sort of problem or game related to the mini-lesson while the teacher confers with individual students or groups of students.
- Reflection or share

This book focuses on one component of your math block—your warm-up, which I refer to as a number sense routine, prior to the mini-lesson. Students need quick, explicit, daily experiences with number sense concepts. Routines provide that structure, no matter what you are teaching during the mini-lesson or during the active learning portion of the math block. The routine does not always need to be related or connected to the math lesson for that day or the math unit for that month. Its purpose is to provide a daily experience with a number sense concept. The ultimate goal is that students make connections over time, build an understanding of relationships among numbers and operations, and ultimately apply their number sense understandings in problem solving.

STUDENTS MAKING CONNECTIONS, UNDERSTANDING RELATIONSHIPS, AND APPLYING THEIR NUMBER SENSE: THE POWER OF NUMBER SENSE ROUTINES

Numerical literacy is the goal. We want students to build number sense and *use* their number sense. I keep my eye on that goal by observing students' number sense growth, then watching for its application to mathematics problems and discussions. All students have their own path as they move toward numerical literacy. Let me share snippets of Jaime's, Margaret's, and Andy's paths.

Jaime

One morning in early May, I began our math class with the following scenario: "We've been working outside in our garden to get it ready for planting. We've talked about how much space we need between seeds. We've also observed other gardens with nice neat rows of plants. We decided our garden will need three rows of five seeds. How many pumpkin seeds will we need?"

Jaime, a first grader, started to solve the problem as he usually did, by directly modeling the situation. He took out the pumpkin seeds one by one and lined up five seeds, then lined up another row of five seeds, and finally lined up a third row of five seeds. After his seeds were organized into three rows of five seeds, he counted all the seeds by ones: "One, 2, 3, 4, 5, 6, 7, 8, 9, 10, 11, 12, 13, 14, 15." However, this time Jaime did something different after counting by ones.

"Hey, that's like 5, 10, 15, like the red and white beads!" he said, referring to the rekenrek, a Dutch arithmetic tool we had been using earlier to explore the power of the five- and ten-structure of numbers (discussed in depth in Chapter 3). This routine provided a visual for Jaime that helped him "see" how numbers are composed. Now he was able to recount the seeds by fives and pointed to each row, saying aloud, "Five, 10, 15, see?!" This was the first time Jaime had applied a more efficient counting strategy to solve a story problem.

This was a great moment for Jaime. Previously he had listened to other students solve problems using the more efficient counting strategy and was able to explain what they did, but he had never applied this more efficient strategy on his own. The daily interaction with number sense ideas affected the way Jaime began to think about numbers. He started to "see" quantities and apply his understanding to solving a problem, thereby becoming more efficient and fluent in his computation. This was a student who was "struggling with number sense." He had strategies to solve problems, but found it difficult to be more efficient. The key in Jaime's evolution of number sense was the daily engagement in routines—and for this specific example, it was the routine of visualizing quantities of fives by using the rekenrek routine and then using this visualization to solve a math problem more efficiently. In other words, the routines allowed Jaime eventually to use his number sense understandings and apply them to a mathematical situation.

Margaret

Like Jaime, Margaret was a student who was struggling. Unlike Jaime's distinct "aha" moment, Margaret's understandings and application of number sense developed over a longer period of time.

It took a while for Margaret to understand Count Around the Circle (discussed in depth in Chapter 4). Eventually, though, this ended up being the routine that helped her develop the confidence to attack even the most daunting math problems. By midyear in third grade, after participating in numerous whole-class and small-group Counts Around the Circle, I noticed that Margaret was finally becoming more fluent with a variety of counting sequences, even when we started at various points (for example, counting by hundreds starting at 347). When asked, "What do you notice about this counting sequence?" she was able to discuss which place in the number was changing and why. This new fluency in counting and understanding of place value was also transferring to her problem solving during the rest of math workshop. She began counting by tens and hundreds rather than by ones. The first time I watched her count backward by hundreds to solve a subtraction problem (*There were 783 books at the book fair and Ms. Lindgren sold 200 of them*), I wanted to jump up and down with joy.

Count Around the Circle had helped her develop a mental number line, understand the patterns of our place-value number system, and use leaps of friendly numbers like 100 and 10 to solve problems. Her ability to problem solve and her confidence in solving math problems skyrocketed as she "got" Count Around the Circle.

Andy

Unlike Jaime and Margaret, Andy had a fairly strong sense of number when he entered my classroom in the fall of his third-grade year. He knew how to decompose numbers and use his understandings of place value to solve problems using tens and ones. He knew how to skip-count by a variety of numbers, which helped him solve multiplication and division problems.

What I observed during our routines (mostly during our discussions about the mathematics in Count Around the Circle and Quick Images with dot cards) was that Andy was growing his number sense in terms of relational thinking. During the number sense routines, Andy was pointing out relationships he noticed among numbers and equations. When we looked at Quick Images with dot cards he eventually started playing with ideas of equality, the distributive property, and the associative property, stating, "Four groups of 3 is the same thing as 2 groups of 6. It just depends on what the story problem is, but you can just take those 2 groups of 3 and make them 6 and take the other 2 groups of 3 and make that 6—either way the total is 12." (See Andy's thinking in Figure 2.2.)

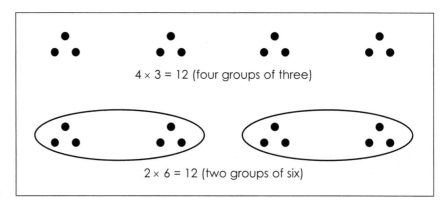

$4 \times 3 = 12$ (four groups of three)

$2 \times 6 = 12$ (two groups of six)

Figure 2.2
Andy's Thinking About Quick Images

Andy practiced his relational thinking as we worked on true/false statements like those that follow. (Note: true/false statements are a number sense routine that is not discussed in this book. For more information, see *Thinking Mathematically: Integrating Arithmetic and Algebra in Elementary School* by Thomas P. Carpenter, Megan Loef Franke, and Linda Levi [2003].)

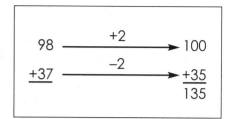

Figure 2.3
Andy's Thinking About 98 + 37

5 + 4 + 10 = 10 + 5 + 5	false
13 + 7 + 4 − 4 = 7 + 13	true
13 + 9 + 6 = 5 + 10 + 13	true
6 + 3 + 10 = 8 + 3 + 7 + 2	false

I observed that he was thinking more and more about relationships among numbers rather than just solving for each side. For example, for the second equation in the preceding list, Andy said he didn't solve both sides because he knew "Four minus four is zero, so that balances the equation."

The more that Andy was thinking relationally during our number sense routines, the more I saw him apply that understanding to other problems. Not only did I watch him use a compensation strategy (which uses relational thinking) in math workshop but I also heard him state a direct connection to the problems we used in our true/false statements: "I know 98 plus 37 is 135 because I moved some of the numbers around like we do in the true/false number sentences. I know that 98 is only two away from 100, and 100 is easier to work with, so I took 2 from the 37 and made it 35. That way 100 plus 35 is 135, and that was easier than 98 plus 37, but it's okay because they mean the same thing." (See Figure 2.3.) Andy was applying what he knew about relationships among numbers and equations to problems such as these. He was becoming more numerically literate due to the variety of routines he experienced each day.

●　●　●

The power of routines that provide students opportunities to interact with numbers, big math ideas, and strategies on a daily basis is exemplified in students like Jaime, Margaret, and Andy. Building number sense every day through routines will improve students' numeracy. By using predetermined sets of routines to enhance the experience in a creative math environment, the teacher sets the stage for successful development and use of number sense.

A LOOK AHEAD

Part II of this book explores ideas for routines I have found to be most effective in helping students build a strong sense of number. The following tables list and summarize the routines that will be discussed in the following chapters.

Chapter 3 **Visual Routines: Seeing and Conceptualizing Quantities**

Name of the Routine	Helps with . . .	How It Works	Ways to Use the Routine and Questioning Strategies
Quick Images Using Dot Cards (and Pictures, Dominoes, and/or Dice) (page 36)	• Subitizing • Visualizing amounts • Using groups and combining groups to figure out "how many"	These are cards with dots on them arranged in various groups. You can make your dot cards based on twos, fives, tens, doubles, or the visual arrangement of dice or dominoes. You flash the amount quickly, giving students about 3–5 seconds to visualize the amount. Then, you ask students what they saw. This will encourage them to think in groups rather than count by ones.	To elicit thinking about Quick Images, ask these questions: • *How many did you see?* • *How did you know it so quickly?* • *Did you need to count? So what did you do? What did you see?* • *Why are you able to know the amount so quickly?* To discuss *perceptual subitizing*, use the following: • 3 dots: *Did you count each dot or did you just see the amount?* • 5 dots: *Did you count? Did you see an amount?* (Some students might see the 5 as a whole amount; others may see 3 and 2 or 4 and 1.) • 3 dots and 1 dot: *How many dots? How did you see it?* • 2 dots and 2 dots: *How many dots? How did you know?* To encourage *conceptual subitizing*, use the following: • 2-by-2 array with 2 dots off to the side: *How many dots? How did you figure it out?* • 5 dots in dice formation with 4 dots in dice formation: *What did you do to figure it out quickly?* • A card arranged with 1 dot, 2 dots, and 3 dots: *How many dots? How did you combine the dots to know how many?* • 4 rows of 3 dots: *How did you know the total so quickly?*
Ten-Frames (page 43)	• Grouping • Using the ten-structure and five-structure • Composing and decomposing ten • Teen numbers • Part-part-whole ideas	You can use the ten-frame much like Quick Images. The difference in using the ten-frame is that the five- and ten-structures are highlighted by the configuration of the frame. The ten-frame can better highlight the idea of teen numbers—the	To elicit thinking about ten-frames, ask the following: • *How did you figure out how many?* To work on *combinations of ten* and the *commutative property*, use problems like these: • 9 + 1 and 1 + 9, 8 + 2 and 2 + 8, 7 + 3 and 3 + 7, etc.

Chapter 3 **Visual Routines: Seeing and Conceptualizing Quantities** *(continued)*

		concept that a teen number is a ten and then some more. The ten-frame can also be used for two-digit addition and subtraction.	To work on *teen numbers*, use the ten-frame to discuss and figure out amounts like this: • Fourteen is composed of a full ten-frame plus a ten-frame with 4 dots. Children can use ten-frames to practice *addition* with problems like this: • A ten-frame with 9 dots plus a ten-frame with 4 dots: Children will often move 1 dot from the 4 to the ten-frame with 9 to make 10, then do 10 + 3. To explore *part-part-whole relationships*, use problems like this: • Show a ten-frame with 6 dots. Ask: *How many dots are needed to make 10?*
Rekenrek (page 49)	• Grouping • Using the ten-structure and five-structure • Composing and decomposing 20 (or 100 on the rekenreks with 100 beads) • Teen numbers • Part-part-whole ideas	The rekenrek is a Dutch arithmetic rack. It has two rows with 10 beads on each (or, on a rekenrek with 100 beads, ten rows with 10 beads on each row). Each row of 10 beads is made up of 5 red beads and 5 white beads. There is a white panel attached to the end of the frame that allows you to hide some beads and show other beads. You can use the rekenrek in a Quick Images manner to encourage the use of groupings. And, like the ten-frame, the rekenrek highlights the five- and ten-structures. The rekenrek is different in that it has 20 beads total (or 100 beads total) and the beads move on the rods, giving it a kinesthetic aspect.	Use these questioning strategies with the rekenrek: • *Can you show a way to make fifteen? Can you show another [a different] way to make fifteen?* • *How many do we need to add to make seventeen?* • *How many do we need to take away to make twelve?* • *What can we do to make eight?* • *How many are hiding behind the white panel?*

Chapter 4 **Counting Routines: Understanding Place Value and the Number System**

Name of the Routine	Helps with . . .	How It Works	Ways to Use the Routine and Questioning Strategies
Count Around the Circle (page 57)	• Counting sequences • Using patterns for problem solving • Estimation • Understanding place value • Understanding how the number system works	Choose a counting sequence—for example, count by tens starting at thirty-two—and go around the circle as each person says a number. (For example, the first person says, "Thirty-two," the second person says, "Forty-two," the next person says, "Fifty-two," and so on.)	Variations on this routine include the following: • Count by ones, tens, fives, twos, threes, and so on, starting at zero. • Count by ones, tens, fives, twos, threes, and so on, starting at various numbers. • Count by fractional numbers. • Count by hundreds or thousands or millions, starting at zero or at various numbers. To facilitate understanding of the patterns, write the numbers on the board as students say them. Ask a variety of questions to differentiate the level of difficulty. (For a list of questions, see Box 4.3).
Choral Counting (page 66)	• Counting sequences • Understanding patterns in numbers	In this routine, the class counts aloud a number sequence all together.	Use this routine if the majority of the class is struggling with the counting sequence. Use a number grid or number line as students are counting to help students see and use the patterns. (See the appendix for various versions of number grids.) To facilitate higher-level thinking and spark discussion about the sequence, ask: *What do you notice about this pattern?*
Start and Stop Counting (page 67)	• Counting sequences • Understanding patterns in numbers • Difference or distance between two numbers	The class counts a number sequence all together, with a starting number and a stopping number. For example, have the class count by tens, starting with 26 and stopping at 176. In addition to whole class, this routine works particularly well with small groups and individual students.	Ask questions to facilitate discussion about *patterns*, such as odd/even patterns: • *If we start with twenty-five and count by fives, what numbers could we stop at?* • *If we count by twos and start with 1,222, what numbers could we stop at? Why would the number need to be even?* To highlight the *distance between numbers* and guide a discussion

Chapter 4 Counting Routines: Understanding Place Value and the Number System *(continued)*

			about *difference*, use the following questions: • *If we count by twos, starting with 1,222 and stopping at 1,234, will it take a long time or not much time? How do you know?* • *If we count by twos, starting with 1,222 and stopping at 4,222, will it take a long time or not much time? How do you know?*
Organic Number Line (page 72)	• Irrational numbers • Various names and representations of numbers • Big ideas like benchmarks, equivalence, the whole, and part of the whole • Strategies like using benchmarks and doubling and halving	This is a number line that you can add to continuously throughout the year. Think of it as one section of your "whole number" number line—you are magnifying (and hence adding more details to) the number line from 0 to 2. For example, there are many numbers that fall between 0 and 1: $\frac{1}{2}$, $\frac{1}{4}$, $\frac{3}{4}$, 0.25, 0.3333, etc. There are also different ways to represent each of these numbers, and some of these numbers are equivalent.	To focus on *benchmarks*, ask questions like these: • *Where does this number go on our number line? How do you know?* • *What numbers can you think of that go between $\frac{1}{2}$ and 1? How do you know?* To focus on *equivalency*, use prompts and questions like these: • *Prove that $\frac{2}{4}$ and $\frac{1}{2}$ are equivalent.* • *Can you show another way to represent $\frac{4}{16}$?* To focus on *the whole and parts of the whole*, ask questions like this: • *Are this half and this half the same amount?* (Show two models representing $\frac{1}{2}$, but each with a different whole.) *Prove it!* To focus on *doubling and halving*, ask questions like this: • *What is half of $\frac{1}{4}$? Where does that fraction go on the number line?*

Chapter 5 **Playing with Quantities: Making Sense of Numbers and Relationships**

Name of the Routine	Helps with . . .	How It Works	Ways to Use the Routine and Questioning Strategies
Ten Wand (page 81)	• Combinations of ten • Commutative property • Part-part-whole ideas • Ten-structure and five-structure	The Ten Wand is made up of ten Unifix cubes, five of one color and five of a different color. The wand breaks in two pieces at various places (decomposing the ten) to help students see combinations visually.	Use questioning strategies like these when working with the Ten Wand: • *How many on the floor and how many in my hand?* • *How did you see seven so quickly? How did you know that's seven without counting it?* • *What is it about the wand that made it easy to see the amount?* • *If we put the parts back together, how many cubes make up the wand now? Why is it still ten?* • *So if there are two on the floor, how many more are needed to complete the broken wand?*
Ways to Make a Number (page 83)	• Thinking flexibly about numbers • Composing and decomposing numbers • Place-value understanding • Base ten and grouping ideas • Relationships among ones, tens, and hundreds	Students write as many ways as they can think of to "make" a selected number. They might use visuals of the quantity, equations, models, and so on.	This routine can be open-ended (just give students the number and no guidelines) or it can have constraints (such as, *Think of ways to make this number with three addends*). Use questions like these with Ways to Make a Number: • *What is it about ten that gave you the idea to write it that way?* • *Why does that work?* • *How do you know it works?*
Today's Number (page 88)	• Understanding numbers embedded in various contexts • Numbers' relationships to 10 and 100 • Grouping ideas (repeated groups, base ten, tens bundled as a hundred)	The teacher chooses a number, such as ten, to be Today's Number (there are a variety of reasons for picking a particular number) and asks various questions about the number, such as: *When is ten big? When is ten small?*	In order to help students understand numbers in various contexts, ask questions like these: • *When is ten a large amount?* • *Why did you think of that as an example of when ten is a large amount?* • *When is ten not very much?* • *Why does ten mean different things in different contexts?* (See Box 5.3 for a complete list of ideas and for questions to use with Today's Number.)

Chapter 5 **Playing with Quantities: Making Sense of Numbers and Relationships** *(continued)*

			To highlight *a number's relationship to 10 and/or 100*, ask questions like these: • *How far is 24 from 100? How do you know?* • *How far is twenty-four from ten? How did you figure it out?* • *How many 24s are in 100?* Use the following questions to elicit discussion about *base ten ideas* in relation to Today's Number: • *How much is ten groups of twenty-four?* • *How many tens are in twenty-four?*
Mental Math (page 91)	• Efficient strategies • Flexible thinking • Place-value understanding • Base ten and grouping • Using relationships among numbers • Computation and operations properties	Present an equation or story problem and ask students to solve it in their heads (without paper and pen or manipulatives). Children should then verbalize the strategies they used mentally.	To facilitate students verbalizing their mental math, use questions like these: • *What did your brain do?* • *Why does that work?* • *Who can restate what Kelly said/did in her head? Why do you think she used that strategy?* • *What part was tricky to do without paper?*

Chapter 6 **Calendar and Data Routines: Using Numbers Every Day**

Name of the Routine	Helps with . . .	How It Works	Ways to Use the Routine and Questioning Strategies
Calendar (page 102)	• Understanding how our time is organized and measured • Counting, recognizing, and sequencing numbers	Use a real calendar in addition to a premade calendar from the teacher store. As a class, write in important days throughout the school year (birthdays, field trips, etc.). Integrate social studies and science.	Questions to use for the calendar routine include these: • *What is today's date? What was yesterday's date? What will tomorrow be?* • *How many days (or months) until Thanksgiving?* • *When did we go to gym class?* • *If January ends on a Monday, on what day will February begin?*
Collecting Data Over a Long Period of Time (page 104)	• Using numbers in authentic ways • Thinking about patterns and cycles • Getting a sense of measurement amounts • Using descriptive statistics	Collect data, such as temperature, weather, and sunrise/sunset times, over time on graph paper in public spaces in the classroom on a daily basis. Once or twice a month, hold class discussions about the data trends and the interpretation and analysis of the data.	Discuss *patterns in temperatures and weather* with questions like these: • *What do you notice about the data? What tells you that?* • *What do you think this graph will look like next month? How do you know?* To encourage the *use of descriptive statistics*, ask questions such as these: • *What is the most common temperature this month?* • *What is the most common type of weather this month?* • *What is the mean temperature in January?* • *What's the range in temperature for September? How is it different from the range in December?* Examine the *visual pattern of sunrise and sunset times* and ask questions such as these: • *What do you notice about the length of the day over time?* • *What patterns do you notice in the data?*
Counting the Days in School (page 109)	• Gaining a sense of growing quantities • Keeping track of information • Thinking about patterns	Use sentence strips and sticky notes to build a number line throughout the year that will emphasize each tenth day of school.	To help students have discussions about the growing quantities and the patterns in keeping track of the days in school, ask questions like these: • *What color sticky note do you need for today? How do you know?* • *How did you know what number comes next?*

Chapter 6 **Calendar and Data Routines: Using Numbers Every Day** *(continued)*

	• Beginning to think about why ten is an important and friendly number	Use a number grid from 1 to 180 to keep track of the days in school. Add one cube to a container each day you are in school (and eventually organize the cubes into tens to count efficiently). Add one rock to a container each day you are in school (see a pile grow).	• *How many days will it be on Friday?* • *Which number on the number grid will we move the circle to on Friday?* • *How many days until the 100th day of school? How do you know?* • *How will you count the cubes?* • *About how much of the rock jar do you think will be filled up by the seventy-fifth day of school?*

PART II

NUMBER SENSE ROUTINES

VISUAL ROUTINES

Seeing and Conceptualizing Quantities

H ow many dots do you see?

You probably did not need to count the dots by ones, but instead saw the amounts in groups. Did you see a group of five and a group of two, then combine them to make seven? Try this one:

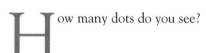

Maybe you saw ten and five or three groups of five in this second illustration. Again, you probably did not count each dot one by one. You were able to recognize small amounts without counting—you were *conceptually subitizing*. Subitizing was something you were able to do early in your path to number sense.

33

WHAT'S THE MATH?

Subitizing

Douglas Clements has written extensively on subitizing. He discusses two types of subitizing: *perceptual subitizing* and *conceptual subitizing*.

Perceptual subitizing is what Layla was able to do. She was able to recognize a small amount without any learned mathematical knowledge.

Conceptual subitizing is what you were able to do with the first two illustrations in this chapter. You identified patterns and groups and saw them as a unit. For example, in the second illustration you either saw a ten and a five or you saw three rows of five. Either way you saw the groups, and you perceived them together as a unit of fifteen.

Clements (1999) explains that subitizing is foundational to children's number sense. He states, "Children use counting and patterning abilities to develop conceptual subitizing. This more advanced ability to group and quantify sets quickly in turn supports their development of number sense and arithmetic abilities" (401).

There are two types of subitizing, perceptual and conceptual. Young children are able to *perceptually subitize*, or visualize and recognize amounts (usually five or fewer), at an early age, before they even know how to count. Later, children are able to *conceptually subitize*, meaning they recognize those small amounts and combine them to see them as a unit. That's what you were doing with seven and fifteen in the two illustrations. In the following vignette, Layla, a kindergarten student, illustrates *perceptual subitizing* (see Box 3.1 for more about subitizing).

One afternoon in October, Layla and I were working on counting small amounts. I gave her four teddy bear counters and asked, "How many bears are here?"

She showed me four fingers and said, "Seven."

"Can you count them?" I asked her.

As she touched each bear, Layla said, "One, two, six, five." She said a number word for each bear, but stopped counting in sequence after two.

"So how many bears are here?" I asked again. Again, Layla put up four fingers. I helped her say each number as she touched each bear: "One, two, three, four."

"So how many?" I asked again.

Layla smiled, put up four fingers, and said, "Seven."

Layla was matching her fingers with the quantity of bears, but when asked how many bears, she was saying the incorrect number. After several similar experiences with her, I realized that she knew the number names (at least she wasn't saying letters!) but did not know which name to assign to which quantity, nor did she say the numbers in the correct sequence. Nevertheless, she could immediately show me an accurate visual representation of the amount with her fingers.

Although Layla was not yet counting, she was visualizing and discerning the correct amount (subitizing). Since I knew she was able to subitize, I needed to build on this strength by providing her more opportunities to do so. This would increase her capacity to subitize (with the goal of being able to conceptually subitize) while also help her learn the names of the quantities and learn to sequence number words. Those were my next steps for Layla (see Box 3.2).

The knowledge of the counting sequences, such as counting by ones or tens, is essential to number sense. It is important for children to have solid counting skills, understand counting sequences, and use patterns within counting sequences (I will discuss this further in the Chapter 4). So, counting is a key component to number sense; however, counting is not enough for children grappling with beginning number concepts. Children need visual, perceptual, and conceptual understandings of quantities. They need images and visual understandings to go with the numerals and the counting words they are learning.

I want to explore here how to build children's number sense by starting with their natural ability to subitize. The routines in this chapter encourage

Using Students' Thinking and Work to Plan Number Sense Routines
Case Study on Layla: Next Instructional Steps

This chart lays out a number sense trajectory for Layla (see Box 1.1 for the definition of each term in this chart). I used this number sense trajectory to help me see what Layla was able to do and to plan the next instructional steps, as described below.

Name of Student	Subitizing	Magnitude	Counting	One-to-One Correspondence	Cardinality	Hierarchical Inclusion
Layla	She is able to use perceptual subitizing. She recognizes amounts of four or less without counting, as evidenced by matching a finger amount to the given quantity. *Next steps:* Continue to provide opportunities to perceptually subitize, and eventually move into routines that will teach her to conceptually subitize.	She has a sense of magnitude. When given two piles, she can compare and tell which has less and which has more. *Next steps:* Once she learns the number names of amounts, she should use those names when she compares amounts (for example, "Five is more than three").	She knows number names, but does not say them in the correct sequence. She does not attach the correct counting names to quantities. *Next steps:* Provide opportunities to count in order. She needs opportunities to count out an amount correctly.	She is able to tag with one-to-one and says a single number name with each tag, but the number name is incorrect.	She does not have cardinality because she does not yet count. She says a number when I ask, "How many?" She knows that the answer is a number.	She does not understand that numbers nest within each other. She does not understand that seven is within eight or that nine is one more than eight. She needs to develop cardinality before she understands hierarchical inclusion.

Layla was perceptually subitizing. She did not have much formal math knowledge, but she could recognize small amounts. As her teacher, I knew I needed to teach from what Layla *could* do in order to strengthen her number sense effectively. She could perceptually subitize, but needed to (1) continue to practice the skill of subitizing, (2) learn the names of quantities, and (3) learn the counting sequence. I planned to use the following routines with Layla in a small group of two to three students, sometimes with the whole class, and sometimes one-on-one during her centers time (when the children have some free exploring time):

- Use dot cards and have her show how many with her fingers.
  - Begin with perceptual subitizing (with dot cards that show from 1 dot up to 5 dots).
  - Gradually incorporate dot cards that encourage her to conceptually subitize (with dot cards that show more than 5, but are grouped in twos, threes, fours, or fives).
- Choral count with her every day using the dot card images in counting order, thereby linking the pictorial quantity with the number name. Show a card with 1 dot and say, "One," show a card with 2 dots and say, "Two," and so on (see illustration to the right).
- Give her dot cards and have her sequence them. Then, point to a card and have Layla name the quantity (and/or write the numeral).
- Use Count Around the Circle with the whole class (see Chapter 4) to help her learn the counting sequence. This will eventually help her attach names to the quantities she knows.

 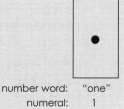 

number word: "one" "two" "three"
numeral: 1 2 3

visual understandings of amounts and support the development of students' thinking about quantities in various groupings. We will look at how mathematical visuals and images bolster the understanding of mathematical concepts like quantity and computation. Visuals and images of amounts help with several learning goals:

- Develop students' understanding of a quantity.
- Give numbers meaning.
- Help students see the relationships of numbers to one another.
- Support an understanding of how numbers operate.

The conceptualization of quantity is foundational to number sense. As students' abilities to visualize amounts improve, their number sense improves. Their strategies and mental math become efficient and quick.

QUICK IMAGES USING DOT CARDS (AND PICTURES, DOMINOES, AND/OR DICE)

Quick Images are pictures of quantities, usually organized in such a way as to encourage students to use, enhance, and build on their subitizing abilities. The teacher shows students a Quick Image for just a few seconds, and then the students try to name the quantity that was shown. The quickness of the routine diminishes the tendency to count by ones. Because you show the image for only a few seconds, children are challenged to conceptually subitize and/or combine groups of amounts. Quick Images set up opportunities for your students to practice thinking more efficiently and automatically about quantities, advancing their mental math abilities. Quick Images routines provide you with opportunities to continually assess how your students are thinking about amounts.

It is easy to differentiate Quick Images routines. Moreover, they can be used for many different purposes, from encouraging the use of subitizing small amounts with kindergartners to visualizing multiplicative ideas with third graders. Although I discuss dot cards here, keep in mind that pictures, dominoes, and dice also have fantastic visual configurations that can be used for Quick Images (see Figure 3.1). In fact, it is important to use a variety of models for the routine. You might plan to use dot cards for three days, dominoes for two days, and some carefully selected pictures organized in arrays for a few days after that. This way your students use similar mathematical ideas within a mixture of formats. Having this assortment of experiences with the visuals helps students think flexibly and encourages deep understanding of subitizing. Also, showing the same quantity configurations in different contexts will let you know if your students' understandings are solid or if they are still fragile and need some support.

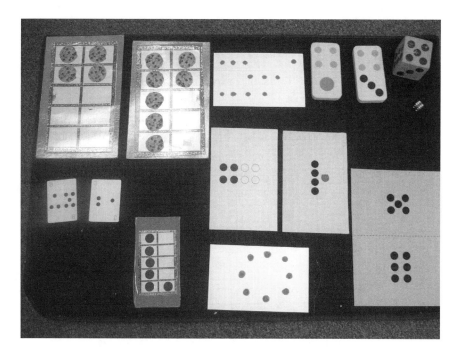

Figure 3.1

Subitizing and Using Groups

Let's dive into how Quick Images work. We will start in a first-grade class-room where we were using dot cards for the first time as the warm-up to our math lesson. I told the students that I would show them a card with dots on it, but I would only give them a few seconds to look at it. When they thought they knew how many dots were on the card, they were to show a silent thumbs-up (in their lap, quietly show a thumbs-up). I flashed the first card, which had 4 dots arranged in a 2-by-2 array:

More than half the class showed a silent thumbs-up.

"You allowed everyone time to think by keeping the amount in your head," I said to the class. "Saying it aloud would have stopped your friends' thinking and you did not do that. What did you see, Ana?"

"Four," Ana answered.

"How did you know it so quickly?" I asked.

"I counted one, two, three, four," Ana explained.

"What did you see, Brandon?" I asked.

"I saw two and then two, and I know two plus two is four," he said.

Differentiating with Dot Card Configurations

I was just starting the Quick Images routine with the first-grade class described, so I used a dot card that was arranged like this:

Same Color or Shading

The dots on this card are arranged in such a way that it encourages thinking about the image as a group of four and a group of two. I might take this scaffolding a step further with a kindergarten class doing Quick Images for the first time. I might instead use the same configuration but have the dots in different shades or colors, like this:

Different Shadings

The shades make the groupings stand out more and encourage the kindergartners to use their subitizing skills.

To make the Quick Image more challenging, I might create a card that looks like this:

Scattered

This more scattered arrangement in combination with the speed of the routine forces students to find their own quick ways to group the amount so they can identify the total. When you use the card in this way, you surely will have more students explain that they see three and three and that makes six, rather than the four and the two. However, you will have some students who still see the four and the two and/or students who count by twos. It is fascinating to try the randomly scattered dots and see that students' brains work differently and group the dots in ways that are easiest for the individual.

"Did anyone see it a different way—different from Ana and Brandon? What about you, Fatima?"

"I just knew it was four."

"What do you mean?" I asked. "Did you count the dots?"

"Nope, I just saw the four," she said.

With just this one card I quickly was able to assess that Ana counted by ones (which made me want to probe a bit further—did she really count them one by one, or did she see the four?), Brandon saw groups of two, and Fatima subitized four. I used the card with only 4 dots to get this kind of information and to emphasize the idea that you don't necessarily have to count to find an amount. Fatima was pretty confident about not counting one by one, but instead visualized the amount as a whole. However, I come across many children who overgeneralize the importance of counting. As teachers, we use questions like *Can you count it to check?* or *Could you count that again?* when in fact, counting is often not the efficient way to figure out how many. It is more efficient to perceptually subitize small amounts, like four, rather than count each item, "One, two, three, four." It is more efficient to conceptually subitize larger quantities and combine groups to figure out the total than to count each item by ones.

Think about it in terms of reading. It is cumbersome and inefficient to sound out every single letter in a word. When children begin to recognize and use chunks of letters within a word or read sight words, they become more fluent readers. This frees up their cognitive energy for more challenging words. It is the same in mathematics. Seeing groups and thinking about amounts in terms of groups leads students to become more fluent and numerically literate. Their cognitive energy can then be spent on more challenging problem solving.

To build on the perceptual subitizing that Fatima and others were doing in this first-grade class, I showed them the next dot card. This time there were 6 dots, with 4 dots again in a 2-by-2 array and the other 2 dots off to the side:

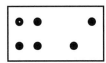

Some students saw the four and the two and some counted by twos. One student said he just saw the six. When I probed further, I found out he actually conceptually subitized the six because he saw three and three. This was interesting, because groupings of two were emphasized by the card's arrangement of dots. He thought he had just seen the six because his brain almost instantly saw three and three as six. I asked the children why they didn't count by ones, but used these other strategies instead. Brian said, "It's faster to do it like four and two. You don't give us enough time to count them all because you turn the card over so fast." For ideas on differentiating with dot cards like those described in this first-grade example, see Box 3.3.

Using Dot Cards for Doubles, Doubles-Plus-One (or -Two), and Doubles-Minus-One (or -Two)

At the beginning of the school year, I realized that about half of the students in my third-grade class were not using doubles to help them with facts that they did not know quickly, like 8 + 7. Instead, for a problem like this, they were counting up from 8. Most knew the doubles facts automatically but were not always using their knowledge of doubles in problems like this. For instance, they would not do either 7 + 7 = 14, so 8 + 7 must be 15 (doubles-plus-one), or 8 + 8 = 16, so 8 + 7 must be 15 (doubles-minus-one). I planned a sequence of dot cards (combined with a specific sequence of ten-frames, which are described later in this chapter) to help my students become more fluent with addition problems in which they could use doubles facts. My hunch was that some of them were not applying their doubles to these addition situations because they were not visualizing what was happening with the quantities. The dot cards would help students see and conceptualize doubles-plus-one or -two and doubles-minus-one or -two. Although that was my main focus for this routine, students who were not well grounded with their doubles also benefited because of the attention and emphasis placed on visual quantities of doubles.

On the other end of the spectrum, some of my students were using doubles to solve addition combinations like 8 + 7 (or had the combination memorized). So, how would this routine build their number sense and challenge them? I relied on them to begin the conversation about using doubles to solve problems, thereby teaching the strategy to the students who were not doing it. Their challenge would be to communicate clearly why such a strategy works, how it works, and when to use it. I also arranged the dots so the children would think of the quantities in flexible ways: the doubles-plus-one and doubles-minus-one strategies; groupings different from the targeted strategy (for example, perceptually subitizing three or four different amounts and combining them quickly); and multiplicatively (for example, seeing equal groups repeated within amounts or arrays). Using a variety of visual arrangements and encouraging children to think flexibly enhances students' visual understandings of the total amount and its parts. For example, look at the dot cards in Figure 3.2.

I had a clear goal for using the Quick Images routine (to help students develop an essential addition combinations strategy), but I also wanted to ensure that I was challenging everyone and helping to build their number sense in the process, even if they were already using this particular addition strategy. To differentiate the routine, I asked questions like, "When does that strategy work?" and "How do you know when to use that strategy?" and "Could you think of another way to look at it?"

I used dot card sequences (sometimes known as "strings") by planning a sequence of specific dot cards. For example, I would show an 8 + 7 dot card

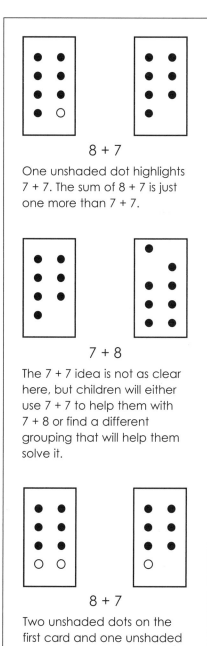

8 + 7

One unshaded dot highlights 7 + 7. The sum of 8 + 7 is just one more than 7 + 7.

7 + 8

The 7 + 7 idea is not as clear here, but children will either use 7 + 7 to help them with 7 + 8 or find a different grouping that will help them solve it.

8 + 7

Two unshaded dots on the first card and one unshaded dot on the second highlight 6 + 6.

Figure 3.2
A Variety of Visual Arrangements Representing 8 + 7

(like those in Figure 3.2), then show a 6 + 5 dot card, and then a 4 + 5 dot card. The dot cards in a sequence are related to one another in order to help students see patterns and relationships among numbers, problems, or equations (for example, the 8 + 7, 6 + 5, and 4 + 5 sequence helps children better see the relationship between a double, like 7 + 7, and a doubles-plus-one, like 8 + 7). We did one or two of these dot card sequences each day at the start of our math workshop for about a week and a half. Then, I continued for a few extra days with a few more dot card sequences with a small group of students who were still not solid with doubles and doubles-plus-one (or minus-one). Using sequences of dot cards each day over a period of time helps students generalize about important number sense concepts and number properties. Keep in mind that each class and every group of students is different. Some may need more time with such a routine; some may need less.

You should also take into account that even when you plan routines with a particular goal in mind, students sometimes take their thinking in a completely different direction. This is when it is especially important to listen to the children—really hear what they are thinking—and plan routines and lessons based on their learning needs. As teachers, it is sometimes difficult to balance these adjustments with the curricular demands, but if we continue to put the thinking back on students and plan lessons responsive to their needs, the results in their number sense will be that much stronger.

Appendix A provides some starting points for encouraging doubles-plus-one and minus-one strategies as well as sequences that encourage other addition strategies and multiplicative thinking. Note that some of the cards in Appendix A, when flashed, will not necessarily work for the purpose of bringing out a doubles-plus-one or minus-one strategy. And that's okay! I developed these sequences with the hope that this strategy would be highlighted. I had a specific goal for my third graders based on a formative assessment of students' needs—I wanted to encourage their use of known facts (in particular, doubles) to solve other combinations with which they were not yet fluent. Sometimes the students saw a card or sequence of cards in a completely different way than I had planned. It was important to listen to their thinking and understand how they were seeing the quantities and thinking about the images so that I could assess their level of understanding. From there I could plan further opportunities to build their knowledge. Also, I had to keep in mind that they were still working on automaticity and visualizing quantities and that efficient strategies come with time and experiences.

Applying Visual Understandings to Efficient Addition Strategies

I worked with a class of second graders during their unit on addition and subtraction early in the school year. During their math workshop time, they were solving problems using two-digit plus two-digit numbers and two-digit

Figure 3.3

minus two-digit numbers. They were involved in drawing pictures, using the number grid, and using base ten blocks to solve the problems. Their teacher and I were impressed with their persistence and with their willingness to grab number grids, manipulatives, or other tools when they needed them (see Figure 3.3).

We encouraged students to use manipulatives and tools during math workshop, but we also wanted to make sure they were building their mental math skills, and expected them to recognize that using mental math on some of the two-digit join and separate problems would be an easier and more efficient strategy. We also noticed that some students were struggling with using the base ten blocks, and we knew that Quick Images would be a better tool to help these students visualize the quantities. We devised Quick Images routines to do each day over a two-week period as the warm-up before their addition/subtraction math workshop. We planned these Quick Images day by day depending on what we observed students do, were on the verge of doing, or needed help learning how to do. In Appendix A, "Dot Card Sequences to Try" shows some of the dot cards we used with these second-grade students, as well as other Quick Images sequences that will help you get this routine started.

Informal and ongoing assessments of students' math strategies drove our instructional plans for this routine. The classroom teacher and I assessed that many students were not using mental math for problems that we thought they could solve easily with mental math strategies. We intended for students to use mental math, and they showed us that they were not readily using this skill. Students need to distinguish when to apply mental math and when to

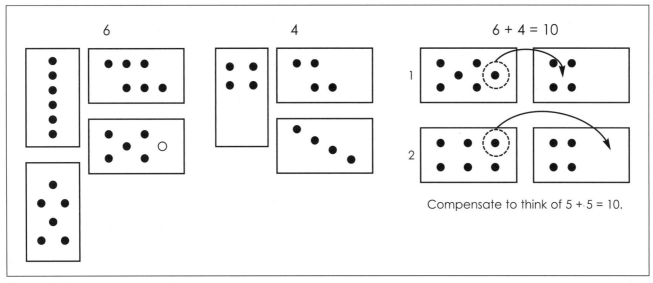

Figure 3.4
Thinking Visually About 6 and 4

use manipulatives like base ten blocks for solving two-digit addition and subtraction problems. Both mental math and manipulatives are appropriate, but we wanted students to more easily identify when mental math would be more efficient and when using manipulatives was a better choice. We chose to use Quick Images to bolster students' visualization of quantities and their mental math with smaller amounts. They in turn started applying their mental math skills to the two-digit addition and subtraction problems. Instead of using base ten blocks for a problem like 24 + 16, they were more apt to visualize the 6 and 4 and see the 10. Their work with 6 and 4 in the dot cards (Figure 3.4) helped them with the two-digit addition problem 24 + 16.

A similar application occurred with problems like 53 + 37. The children were much more solid on combinations of ten, so they quickly recognized and made the group of ten when they saw a 7 and a 3. They could then think about that 10, plus the 50 plus the 30, to find the solution 90. Likewise with the problem 22 + 48. They saw a 2 and an 8 and made 10, and then combined that 10 with the 20 and the 40 to make 70. In the problem 77 − 24, several students cited that they knew what 7 looked like (thinking about 4 dots and 3 dots in dice formation) and were able to visualize the 3 dots missing in the ones place in this problem. So 7 − 4 = 3, and then all they needed to do was think of 70 − 20, which is 50. Therefore, 53 are left.

The Quick Images helped these students build a stronger visual understanding of amounts and relationships among numbers. They were able to apply their mental images of amounts to solving addition and subtraction problems. The children were better able to recognize which numbers were easier to solve mentally (like 53 + 37 and 77 − 24) because they could *see* the amounts and/or combinations of the amounts in their heads.

TEN-FRAMES ROUTINES

A ten-frame is a model that is configured in a rectangular two-by-five or five-by-two array (see Figure 3.5). Like the Quick Images routines with dot cards, routines with ten-frames encourage students to think in groupings and reinforce students' number sense through visual images. But unlike dot cards, ten-frames foster students' development in using the five- and ten-structures of our number system. The ten-frame encourages students to employ conceptual subitizing and also provides a structure that supports students in learning how to work effectively within a base ten number system.

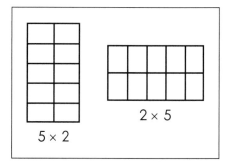

Figure 3.5
Ten-Frames

The structure of the frame always shows a quantity's relationship to ten and allows students to see the "shape" of numbers. It represents the total quantity in such a way that students can see not only the shape of the total amount but also its parts or individual units. This leads students to learn how to compose and decompose ten, and hence, learn the addition/subtraction combinations of ten (see Figure 3.6).

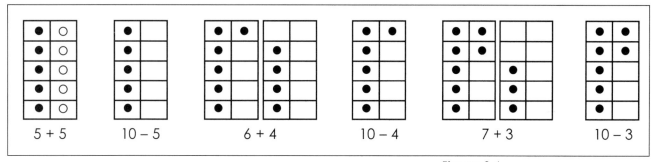

Figure 3.6
Ten-frames help students learn combinations of ten.

The five-structure of the frame—the way that it is always set up in two rows of five—encourages students to use the five to help them figure out how many dots are represented in all. For example, in Figure 3.7, some students will quickly recognize eight in the first frame because they see the five dots on the right side and three more on the left side. Other students might quickly recognize eight because they use the ten-frame to see that there are two missing dots, which means there are eight dots. Likewise, students will quickly recognize the four in the second frame either by subitizing or by seeing that the amount is one less than five.

The structure of the frame teaches students how to compose and decompose ten in a variety of ways because they will visually move the ten-frames' dots around in their heads. In the example in Figure 3.7, students might combine the amounts by moving two of the four dots to the frame on the left in order to make a friendly ten. They compose a ten so that the numbers are easier to work with.

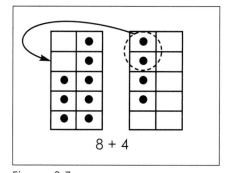

Figure 3.7
The ten-frame helps students see the "friendly ten" strategy. They change 8 + 4 to 10 + 2 to make 12.

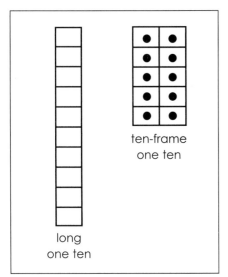

Figure 3.8
The Base Ten Block "Long" or "Ten" Versus the Ten-Frame

When students become fluent with these visual understandings, it is a lot easier for them to use the ten when solving more difficult problems later on. Students who are comfortable with ways to compose and decompose ten are more likely to use the "friendly ten" strategies and the tens and ones strategies.

The visual understanding of ten, supported by the ten-frame, will also help young students grasp the concept of teen numbers more easily. Teen numbers can be the bane of a kindergarten teacher's work. We often see teen numbers represented with base ten blocks to help students see that eleven is one ten and one unit or that thirteen is one ten and three units; however, I will argue that the ten-frame is much more effective, especially when grappling with early number sense ideas. The concept of ten is much easier to see and visually understand on a ten-frame (see Figure 3.8). Have you ever seen young children count and recount the long rod (the ten) of a base ten block? It takes time for them to trust that this will always be ten. Students who have confusions with base ten blocks likely have not yet grasped the concept of unitizing (see Box 1.1, "What's the Math? Early Number Sense Learning Trajectory," in Chapter 1 for a discussion on unitizing). The base ten blocks skip right over the concept development of unitizing, whereas ten-frames provide children time and opportunities to understand ten as one group. Because the ten-frame is structured so that each unit is visually distinct, it is easier to see the quantity that is being represented. The ten-frame is structured in a way that students are less likely to count and recount each time, because they can clearly and instantaneously see the parts of the ten.

Try some routines with ten-frames if your goal is for students to do the following:

- Learn the teen number names.
- Attach the teen number names to the quantities.
- Gain a visual and conceptual understanding of teen numbers.
- Add teen numbers.

You can use ten-frames as Quick Images, like the dot cards, or you can have students sequence ten-frame cards or match ten-frame cards with written numerals. Box 3.4 provides additional ideas for working with teen numbers.

Starting Ten-Frames Routines in Your Classroom

I started a ten-frames routine with a first-grade class using the context of cookies on a cookie tray. Every tenth day of school that year, I dressed up as the Queen of Ten and did a quick activity about the idea of "ten-ness." On the fortieth day of school, I visited the class and showed them my special cookie tray, a large, blank ten-frame. The smiling group of first graders greeted me with the "ten wave," which involved waving both hands to show

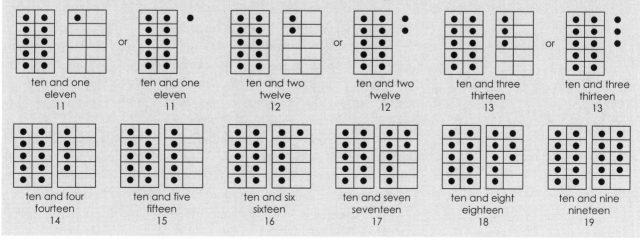

BOX 3.4 Considerations for Teen Numbers and the Ten-Frame

Teen numbers are a difficult part of the number sense journey. This box highlights some of the common problems students have with teen numbers. It also provides ideas for using ten-frames to develop understanding of and fluency with teen numbers. Finally, the illustrations at the bottom give visual examples of ways to set up your representations of teen numbers using ten-frames.

Common Problems with Teen Numbers

Difficulty for kindergarten students:
- Amounts larger than ten become more difficult to keep track of and count accurately with one-to-one correspondence.

Difficulties for young students and English language learners learning teen numbers:
- The number words (*eleven, twelve, thirteen*, etc.) that we use to verbalize numbers are tricky.
  - The linguistic pattern of English does not support the mathematical structure, as it does in some other languages, including Chinese and Japanese. In these languages, the linguistic pattern supports the mathematical structure. For example, if directly translated into English from one of these languages, the name for eleven would be "ten-one" or "ten and one," and the name for twelve would be "ten-two" or "ten and two." Unlike the words in these other languages, the number words we use in English do not help students focus on the ten within the teen number.
  - "Sixteen" sounds an awful lot like "sixty." You will often hear young learners or English language learners count with this sequence: "Ten, eleven, twelve, thirty, forty, fifty, sixty . . ."

Ideas for Using Ten-Frames to Develop Teen Number Concepts and Skills

To help students gain visual and conceptual understandings of teen numbers:
- Have students sequence the teen ten-frame cards (with or without the numeral attached).
- Give students a pile of counters (teddy bears or beans, for example) and two blank ten-frames. Ask students to figure out how many counters they have. The ten-frames can help them visually organize their amount.

To help students learn the teen number names and attach the teen number name to the quantity:
- Show an amount, like twelve, using ten-frames (such as one of those in the illustration below) and have students say the amount. Depending on their level, some students will need to count all the dots by ones. When they do this they are practicing the sequence; over time they will get familiar with the ten-frame and will begin to make sense of the teen concept. Some students will see the ten and the extra dots off to the side and will be able to perceive and say the number.
- Have students match teen ten-frame cards with the written numerals and then have them say the number word aloud.
- Have students match the cards and then sequence them.

To help students add and subtract teen numbers and discuss part-part-whole ideas:
- Show two teen ten-frame cards and ask students to share their strategies for finding out how many altogether.
- Show a teen amount using ten-frames and have students identify the amount. Then, cover some of the dots. Ask students to share their strategies for finding out how many are left.
- Show one or two teen ten-frame cards and ask how many. Then cover some of the dots and ask how many are hiding. Then ask how many are still there. Have students explain their thinking.

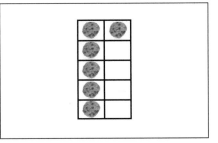

Figure 3.9
My Ten-Frame Cookie Tray with Only Six Cookies Remaining

all ten fingers. "What do you notice about my cookie tray?" I asked them, holding up my ten-frame. Because there were no cookies (dots) on it, they immediately wanted to count the boxes. Several students counted each box with one-to-one correspondence to prove that there were ten spaces. A couple of students got into a discussion about the fact that five boxes on one side and five on the other made ten.

"Well, let me tell you what happened in the land of numbers [where the Queen of Ten lived]. I had one tray, and I baked ten cookies on the tray, with one cookie in each space. But while the cookies were cooling someone ate some of the cookies. Look at this tray." While I was telling them this story I taped six "cookies" to my "cookie tray." I showed them the tray (the ten-frame) with six cookies on it (see Figure 3.9). "How many cookies did she eat?" I asked. Many students were able to see that four cookies were missing. "So how many cookies are still on the tray?" I asked. "How many do I have now?"

"There are six cookies," said Juan.

I encouraged Juan to explain how he saw the amount.

"See, there are five on this side and one more over there. That's six."

"Does anyone understand what Juan saw?" I asked, trying to find out if any students saw it the same way, or if Juan's way was new to them, or if there were students who didn't see what Juan saw at all.

Yesenia restated what Juan saw: "I saw it like that too. He saw those five and then there's one more so he knew there are six cookies."

"Did anyone see it a different way?" I asked. I wanted to spur discussion about other groupings as well as assess what the children in this class were thinking about and if they were seeing the amounts in groups. It is important to hold a discussion among students about the variety of ways they see amounts on the ten-frame in order to help them become more flexible with composing and decomposing amounts.

"I saw three and three," said Jasmine. She showed how she grouped the one by itself with two on the next column, then saw that there were three left over on the top. She said she knew that three and three make six and proved it by representing three plus three equals six with her fingers. In this classroom, Juan was using the five-structure to see six quickly, and Jasmine used equal groupings of threes, thereby using a known doubles fact. Both of these ways of thinking—using the five- and ten-structures and thinking multiplicatively—are important in mathematics because both are cognitive pathways to building strong number sense.

This is one way to start a ten-frames routine and help your students get familiar with the model. Begin the routine much like you would the Quick Images with dot cards. Show the amount quickly (flash a ten-frame with dots in some boxes for only a few seconds). When students explain how they know how many dots are on the frame, listen for and dive into the mathematics (see Box 3.5).

BOX 3.5

WHAT'S THE MATH?

Ten-Frames

The number sense ideas that develop with ten-frames routines include the following:

- Combinations of ten and the commutative property ($9 + 1, 1 + 9, 8 + 2, 2 + 8, 7 + 3, 3 + 7, 6 + 4, 4 + 6, 5 + 5$)
- Visual understanding of the combinations of ten
- Uses of the five-structure (the quinary structure)
  - Seeing seven dots on the ten-frame makes seven easier to work with, because students then think of it as five and two or as a ten lacking three dots on the ten-frame.

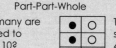

Five and 2 is 7.
Perceive the 5 and 2, then conceptually subitize 7.

- Teen numbers as ten and some ones (fourteen is a ten and four ones)
- Composing and decomposing numbers (seeing groupings within numbers and using groupings to better understand the quantity as a whole and its parts)
- Decomposing and composing numbers to make ten in order to make an addition problem easier
  - The ten-frame helps students clearly see the tens, encouraging them to use place value in addition and combine the tens and then the ones. For example, in the problem $13 + 14$, children may see the two tens clearly and hold 20 in their heads. They can then combine the 4 and the 3 to make 7. All together that makes 27.

Decomposing the Thirteen and Fourteen into Tens and Ones
$13 + 14$

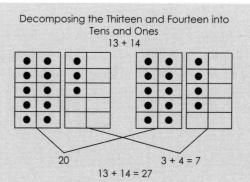

20   3 + 4 = 7
$13 + 14 = 27$

- Compensation strategies in addition
  - The ten-frame helps students visually move dots in order to make a problem easier. For example, $9 + 4$ is made easier because students take 1 from 4 and give it to the 9 to make 10. Then it's visually easier to see that the total amount is 13.

Compensation

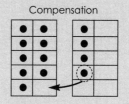

- Part-part-whole relationships

Part-Part-Whole

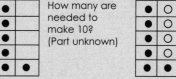

How many are needed to make 10? (Part unknown)

There are 6 shaded dots and 4 that are not shaded. How many dots are there? (Whole unknown)

- Beginning understandings about the base ten number system

Applying Visual Understandings to Efficient Addition and Subtraction Strategies

As you work with the ten-frames on a routine basis, you will see that students get comfortable with ten as a unit (one ten), visually understand how ten is composed (addition/subtraction combinations of ten), use the five-structure to see numbers easily without counting, and decompose and compose numbers more fluidly. For example, a strong visual understanding of "ten-ness" will help students compensate more easily for problems like $56 + 58$. A

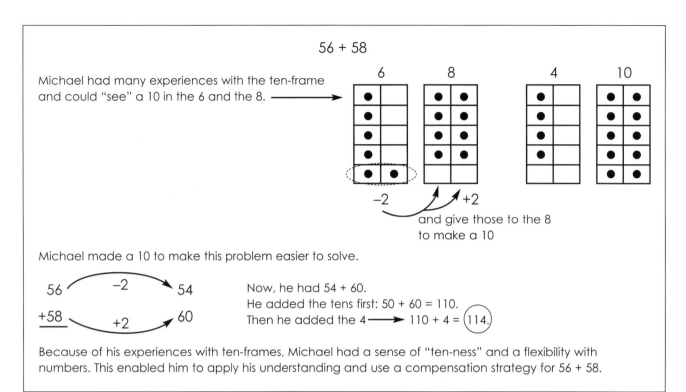

56 + 58

Michael had many experiences with the ten-frame and could "see" a 10 in the 6 and the 8.

6   8   4   10

and give those to the 8
to make a 10

Michael made a 10 to make this problem easier to solve.

56   −2   54   Now, he had 54 + 60.
+58   +2   60   He added the tens first: 50 + 60 = 110.
                      Then he added the 4 ⟶ 110 + 4 = (114.)

Because of his experiences with ten-frames, Michael had a sense of "ten-ness" and a flexibility with numbers. This enabled him to apply his understanding and use a compensation strategy for 56 + 58.

Figure 3.10
Michael's Strategy

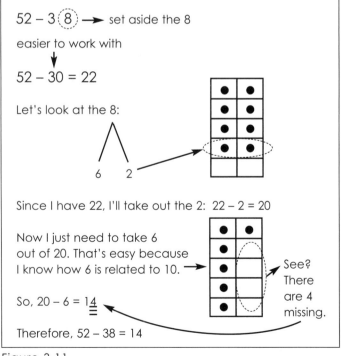

52 − 3 (8) ⟶ set aside the 8

easier to work with

52 − 30 = 22

Let's look at the 8:

6   2

Since I have 22, I'll take out the 2: 22 − 2 = 20

Now I just need to take 6 out of 20. That's easy because I know how 6 is related to 10.

See? There are 4 missing.

So, 20 − 6 = 14

Therefore, 52 − 38 = 14

Figure 3.11
Kelly's Mental Math

second-grade student, Michael, used his knowledge of combinations of ten and solved 56 + 58 using a compensation strategy (see Figure 3.10).

You will also find that because students have played with moving small amounts around on the ten-frames to compose and decompose amounts, they will do this within their mental math strategies, too. For instance, Kelly was able to decompose numbers successfully to solve subtraction problems because she had practiced moving amounts around with the ten-frames. Kelly solved a problem involving 52 − 38 (see Figure 3.11). She took the 8 out of the 38 to make the problem easier. She solved 52 − 30 = 22. Then she decomposed the 8 she took out of 38 to again make it an easier problem. She thought of the 8 as a 6 and a 2. She used the 2 first and calculated 22 − 2 in her head to get 20. Once she had 20, she took out the 6 to get 14. She was able to figure out 20 − 6 quickly because she knew 6 and 4 is 10, therefore 20 − 6 is 14. Kelly's understanding of combinations of ten and her fluency with decomposing numbers helped her solve this problem efficiently using mental math.

REKENREK ROUTINES

The rekenrek, a Dutch arithmetic rack or counting frame, has two rows with ten beads on each row (see Figure 3.12). Each row of ten beads is made up of five red beads and five white beads. You can use the rekenrek in a Quick Images manner to encourage the use of groupings. And, like the ten-frames, the rekenrek has a clear structure and highlights the five- and ten-structures. Also, like the ten-frames, the purpose of the rekenrek is to support students' discovery of number relationships through a clear visual model. The rekenrek also serves as a kinesthetic model, in that students can physically move the beads on the rods (you can also use movement with ten-frames and dot cards by using physical objects with the cards instead of static dots). The rekenrek is different from the Quick Images and the ten-frames in that it usually has 20 beads total (some rekenreks have 100 beads total). Twenty beads help children develop a strong sense of quantity up to twenty as well as automaticity with mental calculation strategies for two-digit addition and subtraction. (Rekenreks with 100 beads take that understanding to the next level, supporting a sense of quantities and combinations up to 100.) A rekenrek is often much easier for young students to use than a number line or number grid, because it is kinesthetic and visual, whereas a number line contains abstract symbols, but the rekenrek supports their understanding of these tools later on.

Watching students' strategies become more efficient as they have multiple experiences with the rekenrek has been eye-opening to me. Second-grade teacher Kassia Wedekind and I used the rekenrek twice a week for two months with a group of twelve students, with the goal of helping them build their number sense and apply more numerically literate strategies to a variety of problems. We started by getting students familiar with the rekenrek through a discussion about it.

Figure 3.12
The Rekenrek (This photo does not show a removable white panel that most rekenreks have attached on the right side. The white panel allows teachers and students to hide some beads and show the rest of the beads in order to represent various quantities.)

"What do you notice?" Kassia asked, holding up a rekenrek.

One student said, "There's red and white."

Another child agreed, then added, "Yeah, and they are the same amount."

"Can someone add on to that observation?" Kassia asked.

Someone else explained, "Well, there are ten beads on top and ten on the bottom, so there are twenty."

The children went on to notice that there were five red beads on the top row and five on the bottom as well as five white beads on the top and five on the bottom, and that all the beads together made twenty. Students often get into some great part-part-whole discussions just talking about what they notice about the rekenrek. This exploration of the rekenrek is crucial to students' understandings of the five- and ten-structures of the tool and how amounts can be composed and decomposed. This type of discussion should be repeated the first few times you use the rekenrek for number sense routines.

Kassia told students that she would show them some beads and hide some beads behind the white panel on one end of the rekenrek. (Rekenreks have a removable white wooden panel at one end so that teachers can hide some beads; this is not shown in Figure 3.12.) She explained that when they knew how many beads were showing, they were to give a silent thumbs-up. We set up the expectations much like I did for the Quick Images routines. We did not quickly flash the beads like we did in Quick Images (although you can do that if you choose to—just use a piece of cloth to cover the beads after you show them for five seconds or so); instead, we observed how quickly or slowly it took students to put their thumbs up. (See Box 3.6 for questions and ideas to use after you have introduced the rekenrek to your students.)

Kassia put all twenty beads behind the white panel and said, "Get your eyes and brains ready." She put out five red beads on the top row. Several thumbs went up right away. A few students nodded their heads each time they looked at a bead, indicating that they were counting the amount by ones. A couple of students thought they saw four, but most said five. Some of the students proved there were five by explaining that they saw three and two, so that made five.

After the class agreed that there were five beads showing, Kassia tried the next round. She displayed all ten beads on the bottom rail. Quickly, several students were able to say there were five red beads and five white beads so there were ten altogether. A couple of students said they just knew it was ten. Others were not quite convinced that there were ten without counting by ones. Kassia and I were not very concerned about the children who were counting by ones—we kept in mind that the children would become more efficient and automatic through the consistent interaction with the routine and conversations with their peers. Becoming more efficient is a natural part of getting familiar with the routine and the ideas and concepts it presents.

Ideas to Get You Started with the Rekenrek

Questions
- How many total do you see?
- Can you show a way to make fifteen? Can you show another way to make fifteen?
- How many do we need to add to make seventeen?
- How many do we need to take away to make twelve?
- What can we do to make eight?
- How many are hiding behind the white panel?

Quantities to Try
Combinations of ten:
Working on combinations of ten with the rekenrek will help students gain automaticity with combinations of ten. The visual images will develop their sense of "ten-ness." Seeing and discussing the groupings will develop their flexibility with numbers. In addition, the red and white beads and the ten beads on each rail will encourage students to use the five- and ten-structures in the way they see and think about quantities. Try the following combinations of ten with the rekenrek:
- Display five reds and five whites on top.
- Display five reds on top and five reds on the bottom.
- Display nine beads on top and one bead on the bottom.
- Display four beads on top and six beads on the bottom.
- Ask students for ways they could make ten.
- Show an amount, such as eight beads, and ask the children how many more they need to make ten.

Amounts in the teens:
Using the ten and some extras will help students develop conceptual and spatial understandings of quantities in the teens:
- Display two beads on top and ten beads on the bottom.
- Display ten beads on top and five beads on the bottom.
- Display ten beads on top and four beads on the bottom.

Compensation strategies:
During discussions about the amounts on the rekenrek, watch for opportunities to have conversations about the compensation strategy. The following ideas might encourage students' compensation strategies to come up in discussions about the rekenrek amounts:
- Display nine beads on top and two beads on the bottom (watch for compensating; some students will visualize one of the beads on the bottom moving to the top to make a ten, so one will be left on the bottom and that makes eleven).
- Display five beads on top and nine beads on the bottom.
- Display eight beads on top and three beads on the bottom.

Part-part-whole, with twenty being the whole amount:
Use the white panel to highlight part-part-whole relationships. Have students think about twenty as the whole amount. Then try the following to discuss the parts of twenty:
- Display ten beads and ask how many are missing (each time, ask students to prove how they know).
- Display fifteen beads and ask how many are missing.
- Display five beads and ask how many are missing.
- Display twelve beads and ask how many are missing.

Kassia continued with fifteen (ten on the bottom row of the rekenrek and five on the top), then fifteen again (with ten on the top this time and five on the bottom). This helped us find out whether the students were counting by fives easily or using the ten and the five.

Later, the students worked on the following problem during math workshop, and we observed to find out if they were using the five-structure mentally:

Last summer, Maria went to Mount Vernon with her class.
She saw 10 pigs, 5 horses, and 15 cows.
How many animals did she see?

Rosa solved this problem mentally and explained, "I just added the 5 to the 15 and saw 20. Then I added the 10 to make 30."

I asked her, "What do you mean you 'saw' 20 after you added the 5 to the 15?"

"It's like moving the white beads over to go with the red. That's a ten," she responded. "If there's 10 on the bottom and 10 on the top, that's 20." She was visualizing the amounts in her head as she solved the problem. In addition, she started the problem with the 5 and 15—she looked for amounts that could be combined to make the problem easier to work with. Once she had 20, it was easier for her to add the 10 pigs to that amount.

Your daily math routines do not always have to be related to your mini-lesson or to the work students are doing in math workshop, but it is important to observe students' applications of concepts and strategies to problems. For many students, we need to help them make connections by making the connections explicit. You can do this without taking from them the responsibility of doing their own thinking. When they are working on problems, prompt them to remember the kind of thinking they were doing during the

 Resources for Quick Images and Other Routines Using Visual Representations of Quantities

BOX 3.7

For more ideas or premade cards, simply use an Internet search engine for "dot cards." John Van de Walle's (2007) book *Elementary and Middle School Mathematics* has black-line masters for dot cards and provides further information about dot cards and ten-frames. The books in Catherine Fosnot and Maarten Dolk's (2001a, 2001b, 2002) Young Mathematicians at Work series have resources on using mini-lessons to build number sense. Some lessons in these resources contain more complex and complicated arrays and arrangements that you will not want to use as "quick" images; it's helpful to leave them up on the board and discuss the different ways of figuring out the quantities. Many of these more complex arrays and arrangements encourage specific ways of grouping or specific strategies, but they are open-ended enough that there are several ways to group or figure out the larger quantity.

Similarly, you will find related ideas in many of the books by Greg Tang, such as *The Grapes of Math* (2001) and *Math-terpieces* (2003). I read and discussed both of these books (a couple of pages each day) with my third-grade class over a two-week period. Our discussions about the images in the books were grounded within two main themes: quickness and efficiency. Students noticed that the more we challenged ourselves with the images, the easier it became to think about groupings. As their abilities to group became more automatic, they realized that some groupings were more efficient than others. They saw that some groupings led to better organized strategies.

These resources and books helped me extend many of the ideas and concepts that came out of the visual routines in my classroom. There are many resources out there that offer great ideas for using visual images in routines or for extending the ideas and concepts that come up in your classroom discussions and your students' work. I encourage you to research them and share what you find with colleagues.

routines by saying, "During our warm-up routine this morning you were counting by fives with the rekenrek. Do you remember what you did? I wonder if that would help you with this problem." With this kind of prompt, you are making the link for them, but they still need to think through the problem.

Although routines do not necessarily need to be related to the work you do during the rest of your math lesson, it is helpful to relate them once in a while (just as we related the problem about Mount Vernon to our rekenrek routine), either as a formative assessment or with the goal of helping students make the connections to their written work. After all, that is the goal of the routines—we want our students to be numerically literate.

When students make the connections on their own and apply key number sense concepts, it is important that they share this strategy and newly acquired understanding during the reflection part of math workshop. The verbal explanation of the strategy will solidify it for the child who is sharing as well as help other children in the class learn the strategy and/or make the leap from understanding the strategy to applying it independently.

FINAL THOUGHTS ABOUT VISUAL IMAGES OF QUANTITIES IN MATHEMATICS

When I first started my career as a second-grade teacher, I often left out the visual part of mathematics. I think that visualizing is commonly overlooked, and we tend to focus on computing with manipulative objects (including counters or base ten blocks) and counting. Counting does not mean much to young children if they do not have the visual images to go with the number words or written numerals. Also, many children seem to lack a visual framework for quantities. They have a difficult time organizing amounts in their heads, and later that leads to difficulties with computation, mental calculation, using efficient strategies, and having clear understandings of number properties and the base ten number system. Visualizing quantities truly is a key component to children's early understandings of number and the application of number sense concepts later on. The visual understandings help them think about the amounts conceptually in addition to symbolically and abstractly. See Box 3.7 for additional resources that give ideas for developing visual and conceptual understandings of amounts.

Children will make leaps and bounds of improvement in number sense as you provide opportunities for them to strengthen the following:

- Visual understanding of quantities
- Ability to think within five- and ten-structures
- Sense of the shapes of numbers within groupings or the ten-frame
- Conceptualization of how quantities are composed and decomposed

As my third-grade student Anthony often told our class, "I always try to *see* the ten because it makes it faster to do in my head."

4

COUNTING ROUTINES

Understanding Place Value and the Number System

Try solving this problem mentally:

Luis had 34 playing cards.
His friend gave him 20 more.
How many does he have now?

Second-grade students might solve the problem in several different ways (see Figure 4.1). Some would solve it by decomposing the 34 into 30 and 4, then combining 30 and 20 to make 50, then adding the 4 back on. Others might count up by tens, saying, "Thirty-four, forty-four, fifty-four." Other students might use the jumping by tens strategy, but might struggle with doing it mentally and need to see those jumps on the number grid or the number line. And there are still other students who would count up by ones. Time and again I find that students who count by ones do not use the more sophisticated strategies (using tens and ones or counting on by jumps of ten) because they are not fully comfortable with skip-counting, nor do they

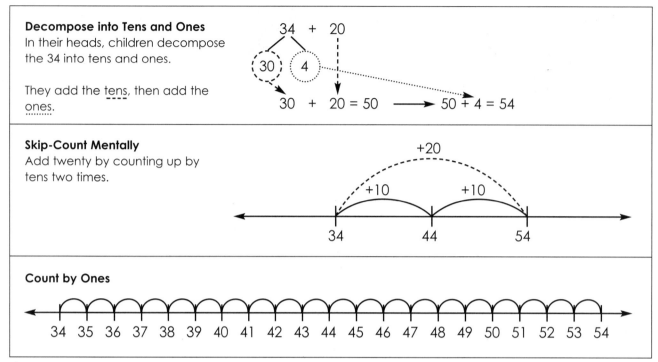

Decompose into Tens and Ones
In their heads, children decompose the 34 into tens and ones.

They add the <u>tens</u>, then add the ones.

$$34 + 20$$

$$30 + 20 = 50 \longrightarrow 50 + 4 = 54$$

Skip-Count Mentally
Add twenty by counting up by tens two times.

Count by Ones

Figure 4.1
Strategies Children Use for Mentally Solving 34 + 20

see the patterns of ten on the number grid. Another reason may be that they do not have mental images of the quantities, as discussed in Chapter 3.

Students who struggle with mathematics often lack counting skills. They might not know the number sequence and/or how to skip-count; they might not have visual models of amounts as they count; and/or they might not understand patterns in place value. Counting is not just a memorized sequence. Counting is putting a name to the quantities, understanding the way our number system is organized, and using patterns (see Box 4.1 for an early counting learning trajectory). Counting sequences help children understand relationships among numbers and further develop their abilities to apply these understandings to problem-solving situations.

The counting sequences we typically teach students in the early elementary grades are counting by ones, tens, fives, twos, and hundreds. Eventually we lead them to become familiar with other sequences, such as counting by threes and fours, and using doubling patterns.

Children need repeated exposure to and practice with counting sequences in order to become fluent with counting. Counting routines provide opportunities for students to create the anchors they need for solving problems efficiently and for doing the math mentally.

The objectives for routines that build counting proficiency are to: (1) understand counting sequences, (2) solidify fluency with counting sequences through recognizing and using counting patterns (usually involving place-value and base ten ideas), (3) practice estimation, and (4) use additive and multiplicative ideas. While working on these objectives, students naturally become acquainted with the number system and its structures, thereby gaining a stronger sense of how numbers work.

COUNT AROUND THE CIRCLE

Count Around the Circle is a routine that involves whole-class participation, with each person saying a number as you count around the circle. To begin, choose a counting sequence; for example, count by tens starting at thirty-two. Have one child start with thirty-two, and go around the circle as each person says a number. (The first person says, "Thirty-two," the second person says, "Forty-two," the next person says, "Fifty-two," and so on). When you introduce the routine for the first time, it is best to start with simply counting by ones. Have one student start with one; the next person should say, "Two," the next person "Three," and so on, until you get all the way around the circle and everyone has said a number aloud.

Count Around the Circle is a whole-class effort and it takes a team to do this routine effectively. It may take several days to establish the procedures before you get into the heart of the mathematics with this routine. Start by setting the following expectations:

1. Everyone needs to listen to each person and count in their heads as each person says his or her number. (This means that everyone is actively participating, even when it is not their turn to say the number.)
2. Give everyone some think time when they need it. (Children inevitably will get stuck and just may need some think time before others help—it's a natural reaction from children and teachers alike to want to help right away. Take a look at Chapter 7 to get ideas for establishing think time.)

Sometimes balancing the think time and keeping the counting going is difficult. At times I have found that I started a counting sequence that was too difficult for the majority of the class. Once, in a first-grade classroom, I asked students to count by fives around the circle, and about a third of the way around the circle (at around thirty-five), I realized that a majority of the students were not solid with skip-counting by fives. Some of the students had strategies for figuring out what came next; however, they were not yet fluent with the counting sequence by fives. In cases like this, which can become a management issue, I often make one of two decisions: (1) I stop the Count Around the Circle and move into Choral Counting, in which we all count the sequence together as a class (sometimes using a number line or number grid for extra visual support), or (2) we stop and discuss as a class what each student will say as he or she counts around the circle, so each student is prepared when it's his or her turn. Then, we start Count Around the Circle all over again. This way the children are still clearly hearing the pattern that

BOX 4.1

WHAT'S THE MATH?

Early Counting Learning Trajectory

Douglas Clements describes a developmental sequence that children go through as they learn to count. Breaking down the learning trajectory into these guideposts helps us analyze students' progress and better plan learning experiences along the way.

Precounter: Says some number words.

Chanter: Says some words in sequence ("singsong").

Reciter: Says number words in sequence (does not need song).

Corresponder: Counts correctly using one-to-one correspondence up to at least five objects, but does not yet employ cardinality when asked, "How many?" (see Chapter 1, Box 1.1, for information on cardinality).

Counter to five: Counts one to five objects meaningfully (now using cardinality).

Producer: Counts out a collection up to five.

Counter to ten: Counts one to ten objects meaningfully.

Counter and producer (more than ten): Counts higher than ten, even when counting unorganized objects.

Counter from *n* (can begin counting at various starting points).

Counter on using patterns.

Counter on keeping track.

Counter forward and back.

(Clements and Sarama 2009)

BOX 4.2

Getting Started with Count Around the Circle: Sequence Suggestions

As you begin establishing the Count Around the Circle routine, these suggestions will give you a place to start:

- Count by ones, tens, fives, twos, threes, etc., starting at zero.
- Count by ones, tens, fives, twos, threes, etc., starting at various points.
  - Count by tens, starting from 320 (320, 330, 340, 350, 360, 370 . . .).
  - Count by tens, starting from 53 (53, 63, 73, 83, 93, 103, 113 . . .).
- Count backward by ones, tens, fives, and twos, starting at various points.
  - Count backward by tens, starting from 110 (110, 100, 90, 80 . . .).
  - Count backward by tens, starting from 322 (322, 312, 302, 292 . . .).
- Count by halves (0, $\frac{1}{2}$, 1, $1\frac{1}{2}$, 2, $2\frac{1}{2}$, 3 . . .), starting at zero or at various points ($16\frac{1}{2}$, 17, $17\frac{1}{2}$, 18 . . .).
- Count by fourths, eighths, thirds, or sixths, starting at zero or at various points.
- Count by wholes, starting at a fractional number.
- Count by hundreds or thousands or millions, starting at zero or at various points

goes around the circle, but they have had a chance to rehearse their number before doing it quickly around the circle. See Box 4.2 for some counting sequences to start with in your classroom.

So how do you know which counting sequences to use? And when is it useful to use a routine like Count Around the Circle? Carrie Cantillana, a second-grade teacher, encourages her students to use strategies that make sense to them and encourages the use of multiple strategies. One year in early winter, she recognized that several of her students were using only one strategy for solving a problem. These students were not only relying solely on the number grid but also were still counting by ones on the number grid. Naturally, they were also struggling to solve problems mentally. Carrie was stuck. She thought this was okay during the beginning of second grade, but she also felt that her students should be moving into more efficient strategies by now. She struggled with whether to give them more time or to plan activities to help them ratchet up their strategies a notch. As we looked closely at students who were relying on the number grid or still counting by ones, we saw that they were not always skip-counting effectively and that they definitely were not applying the skip-counting they knew in order to solve mental math problems.

Carrie and I discussed using the Count Around the Circle routine every day at the beginning of their math workshop for two weeks in order to build the skills for using skip-counting and tens and ones in problem solving. We decided to plan this as a whole-class routine that we would do as the warm-up to math workshop because we had three differentiated objectives. One group of students needed opportunities to practice the counting sequence and apply rote counting to problem-solving situations. Another group of students did not necessarily need the counting sequence, but would be challenged by explicitly explaining their thinking about the counting sequence patterns and how they applied these patterns to problem-solving situations. This group (as well as the whole class) also needed practice with estimation, and we would provide opportunities for estimation during these Count Around the Circle routines through questions before counting (see Box 4.3). A third group of students were fairly solid with using counting sequences or tens with addition but needed a boost with applying these strategies to subtraction. The purpose of our planned counting sequences for these students was to help them with subtraction strategies.

Carrie and I chose to start the first day with counting by ones so we could focus on establishing the expectations for this routine. First we started at one, which prompted students to recognize that there were nineteen people in our circle that day. Then we asked, "What if we went around a second time? What number would we end with?" That gave Carrie and me the opportunity to assess who could double nineteen and how they doubled it, who estimated, and who tried to count by ones. In other words, a question like this during the routine allows teachers to assess students quickly and informally.

In the first few days of the routine, we began each math workshop by "warming up our math brains" using Count Around the Circle. We continued to count by ones for several days, beginning at various starting points: 34, then 97, then 292. This allowed us to solidify the expectations for the routine and build a supportive community that provided think time for everyone and that engaged in math talk with one another. It does take practice to give one another think time and keep everyone engaged! The sequence of counting by ones with starting points at 97 and 292 also let us know if counting by ones into the next hundred was difficult for anyone (for example, 97, 98, 99, 100, . . . and 292, . . . 299, 300 . . .).

Next we counted by tens starting at 10, then counted by tens starting at various numbers. We always started at decade numbers (such as 90 or 220). After the routine was solid and we had gathered more informal data about Carrie's students' counting skills and knowledge of patterns, we were able to plan counting sequences to help her students problem solve more efficiently and become more confident using mental math. Here are the counting sequences we planned for the first six math sessions for Carrie's class:

Days 1 Through 3

- Establish the routine of Count Around the Circle using the counting sequences of ones and tens. For the purposes of assessing students and establishing the routine, start with a count by ones, beginning at various starting points: 34, then 97, then 292. For sequences counting by tens, start with decade numbers (such as 90 or 220), then try other starting points that are not decade numbers (such as 93 or 226).

Day 4

- Count by tens starting at 23 and write the sequence on the board.
- Count by tens starting at 47, without writing the sequence on the board (unless several still need the support of the numerals written on the board or on a number grid).

Day 5

- Count by tens starting at 5, without written support.
- Count by tens starting at 95, without written support.
- If time allows, try these:
  - Count backward by tens starting at 90 (for our group that needs the counting sequences for subtraction).
  - Count by fives starting at 5 (assess to see how students do with fives).

Day 6

- Count by tens starting at 40. Count by tens starting at 140.
- Count by tens starting at 42. Count by tens starting at 342.
- Count backward by tens starting at 94.

BOX 4.3 Questions for Differentiation with Count Around the Circle

To make the Count Around the Circle routine rich enough for all students to have access to it and to be challenged by it, differentiate your questions for students based on their strengths and needs. Here are some ideas:

- Estimation: *If we count by ones starting with Kelly and go all the way around the circle, what number do you think Amir will say?*
  - Emphasize estimation. Take note of kids who are not counting by ones around the circle to figure out the answer to your question, and ask those students how they estimated: *If you didn't count to figure it out, what did you do in your head?*
- Estimation: *If we count around the circle by tens and we go around three times, what will Lucy say? How do you know that without counting it?*
- Estimation: *Why did you choose _____ as an estimate?*
- Estimation: *Why didn't anyone choose _____ as an estimate?* (Pick a number that is not reasonable and that was not offered by a student, and discuss what makes it an unreasonable estimate.)
- Noticing patterns: *How did you know what comes next?*
- If a child became stuck, but figured it out: *I noticed that you paused when it was your turn and then you figured it out. What did you do to figure it out?* (The purpose of this question is to highlight the effective strategy the student used to get "unstuck," with the intention that this particular student, as well as others, will use patterns or relationships to figure out what comes next in the counting sequence.)

Please note that we planned days 4 through 6 based on days 1 through 3 and on the original objective of helping students gain more efficient mental math strategies using tens and ones or counting up by tens. Just as with any math routine, although it is important to be well prepared, you also need to be flexible with your plans and adjust based on your observations, ongoing formative assessments, and students' needs. All that said, the counting sequences we planned are only an example. The routine can take off in many different directions, depending on your class of students. I hope these examples help you find a place to start with your students and see how to build on to the previous days' experiences.

As noted in the discussion about the objectives of the Count Around the Circle, these counting sequences were developed to help build counting proficiency for students who were solving problems like 34 + 20 by counting up by ones rather than by using more efficient strategies like skip-counting by tens or using tens and ones. In addition to this objective for this particular group of students, we were able to challenge other students' thinking by asking estimation questions and computation questions and by facilitating discussions about patterns and place-value ideas that show up while counting (see Box 4.3 for estimation questions). In short, a routine like Count Around the Circle can build hooks for students who need practice counting and also challenge students to estimate, compute mentally, and notice relationships among numbers.

As we used Count Around the Circle as a daily warm-up over those two weeks, we watched for students' application of these skills when they were problem solving. Two students in particular, Maria and George, who were clearly struggling with counting sequences in the beginning, better understood counting by tens by the end of week two and were on the verge of applying this understanding to problem solving.

During the second week of Count Around the Circle, we were using counting by tens at various starting points. When I met with students in a small group for problem solving, I continued to have them practice this type of sequence with the number grid. They would count by tens with the number grid as a visual support and then would try counting without looking at the grid. One day that week, Maria easily counted, "Twenty-seven, 37, 47, 57, 67, 77," for the first time without looking at a written sequence or the number grid.

"How did you know what came next?" I asked her. I wanted to tap into her metacognition and help her reflect on her success.

"When you said tens and start with twenty-seven, I could see the pattern like on [the number grid]," she explained. Maria had started internalizing the sequence.

Later that week George solved this problem mentally:

Lyly had 12 books. Zindy gave her 20 more books.
How many does Lyly have now?

He started at 12 and counted by tens twice (22, 32). Before we provided George opportunities to practice counting by tens, he had automatically reached for the base ten blocks or used the number grid. Carrie wanted to be sure that he would do mental math for problems like this and would only use the tools for problems that were more difficult to do mentally. He solved 12 plus 20 in his head within the context of a story problem, applying number sense ideas.

Another objective for using Count Around the Circle at the beginning of Carrie's math workshop was for students to try a counting (or jumping) by tens strategy with subtraction problems. We hoped they would move away from counting back by ones, a less efficient strategy. Carrie and I created some mental math problems to go with our Count Around the Circle routine and were more explicit in encouraging students to give the strategy a try. "You just counted back from 92 by tens. Let's look at what you just did," I said. Students looked at the chalkboard where I had written *92 82 72 62* . . . all the way down to *2*. "What do you notice?" I asked. After some discussion about the patterns and the counting sequence, I asked them to try this problem in their heads:

> Ms. Cantillana had 92 rocks. She gave 30 rocks to Ms. Riggs. How many rocks does Ms. Cantillana have now?

This problem was still difficult for many students. Marcos solved the problem in his head and explained his strategy of counting back by tens (he started with 92 and counted 82, 72, 62), but students struggled to restate what he had explained. When he explained it with the number grid, it was clearer for more students, but it was apparent to Carrie and me that this was something her students should continue in daily routines. They needed some more time with counting backward. Many were on the verge, but they needed more experiences to solidify the skill.

As you get going with the Count Around the Circle routines, you will find that your students may need sequences or questions to challenge them (see Box 4.3 for ideas). At times you will find that they need additional supports. Use the number grid with students who are really struggling to participate in a particular counting sequence. The number grid will scaffold their counting by helping them see the visual pattern of the sequence. After you've used the number grid for a while, take it away to see if they can count without it. The scaffold is important if students are having trouble seeing the patterns. However, the purpose of Count Around the Circle is to help students become more automatic and independent with counting patterns by having the sequences in their heads. It may take some students more time to be comfortable with skip-counting without the number grid and to really understand the sequence. Again, in these cases, practice with the number grid, then practice without it. Use visuals from Chapter 3 as well as manipulatives or other models and representations in these cases.

Writing Numerals with Count Around the Circle

Let's take a closer look at the visual support of writing numerals on the board during Count Around the Circle. This support provides students with a visual representation of what is going on in their heads. Great discussions about relationships among numbers arise from this added visual support, especially if you are thoughtful about the way you write the sequence as students count. The way you write the sequence as students count will bring up different patterns and ideas for discussion. Think about your objectives for the routine as you plan how to write the sequence on the board:

- For counting by tens, students notice different relationships or patterns when you write the sequence vertically versus when you write it horizontally (see Figure 4.2).
- With Carrie's class, although we were focusing on counting the sequences in our heads (without using the number grid and without writing the numerals), I did decide to write the numerals when we counted by ones starting at 97. I did this because a few students struggled with decade numbers, and the visual would be a good support as we counted over 100. It would also facilitate a discussion about place value and which digits were changing. I debated using one of the three options shown in Figure 4.3. I decided on the list format because I wanted the students' eyes to move down vertically to see how the tens change after every decade number. The vertical list lines up the place values, meaning all the ones are in the right column, the tens are in the middle column,

10	20	30	40	50	60	70	80	90	100
110	120	130	140	150	160	170	180	190	200
210	220	230							

Children tend to notice that the ones and tens stay the same, but the hundreds change as you go down each column. The tens change as you move horizontally.

10	110	210	Children tend to notice that ones and hundreds stay the same, but the tens change as you go down each column. The hundreds change as you move horizontally.
20	120	220	
30	130	230	
40	140		
50	150		
60	160		
70	170		
80	180		
90	190		
100	200		

Figure 4.2
Writing Numerals with Count Around the Circle

Number Line Format

97 98 99 100 101 102 103 104 105 106 107 108 109 110 111 112 113 114 115

List Format	Number Grid Format								
97							97	98	99	100
98									
99	101	102	103	104	105	106	107	108	109	110
100	111	112	113	114	115				
101									
102									
103									
104									
105									
106									
107									
108									
109									
110									
111									
112									
113									
114									
115									

Figure 4.3
Three Options for a Visual Support for Counting by Ones Starting at 97

and the hundreds are in the left column. When the place values are lined up in this way, students can focus in on what is happening in each place-value column. I thought that the vertical pattern would support them with other sequences that contained 99 and leapt into a different set of hundreds because they could clearly see that the hundreds place changes. The place-value columns support that focus more so than some of the other formats.

- Figures 4.4 and 4.5 show two other examples of times when I decided to write the numbers on the board while students were counting. After the

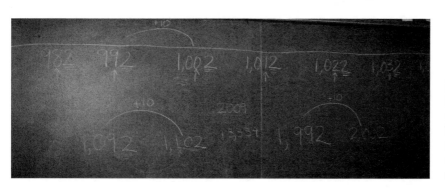

Figure 4.4
We counted by tens, and my students struggled with 1,092 + 10. That discussion led us to a discussion about what 1,992 + 10 would be. The counting and place-value ideas get really tricky there!

Figure 4.5
We counted by 0.25. That led us to a discussion about the whole (1.00, 2.00, etc.) and money, which then led us into a discussion about half of 0.25. At that point in the year (the end of third grade), my students were playing around with relationships between fractions and decimals. The routine set them up for yet another discussion about these relationships.

counting, we analyzed patterns, discussed what was happening in the counting sequence, and applied the ideas to other number sense problems we had been working on.

I ask, "What do you notice?" each time I write out a sequence. This helps students get into the habit of mind of looking for patterns and taking note of relationships among numbers and amounts. It also invites students to think beyond the numbers. Sometimes their "noticings" open up teaching points I had not previously planned. I pursue these teaching points because students are showing me they're ready to learn something new.

Sometimes students need to practice counting sequences in their heads. Sometimes they need to count while using or analyzing a visual. Writing the numbers on the board as students count around the circle will highlight important patterns and relationships, as well as assist some students in learning the sequence through a visual representation.

Listen for Big Number Sense Ideas That You Didn't Plan For

It is great fun and highly beneficial when spontaneous discussions arise from Count Around the Circle. One instance when this occurred was when I was using the routine with a second-grade class. We were working on getting a better sense of quantities and using estimation. The students needed practice counting by tens and fives. My plan included the following Count Around the Circle sequences:

- Counting by ones. First ask students to estimate: "If I start and we go all the way around the circle counting by ones, what do you think the last person will say? Try not to count. Think about it in any other way without counting." Count around the circle, then have students check their estimates (just with an individual reflection). Finally, ask students to estimate again: "Okay, so we landed on twenty. What will the last person say if we go around one more time?"
- Counting by tens. Ask, "If I start again and we go all the way around the circle counting by tens, what do you think the last person will say?" Go through the same procedure of focusing on good estimates. Ask questions about ridiculous estimates: "Why didn't anyone estimate thirty? Why didn't anyone say a million?"
- Counting by fives. Continue with the preceding questions.

When we tried out this plan, students' estimates were pretty solid when we counted by ones. Many of them thought about the number of students in the class and made an estimate close to twenty. When I asked them to estimate what the last person would say if we went around again, several were able to say "forty" and explain their strategy. We discussed why more estimates were exact answers this time around (because many of them doubled what we had landed on).

When I had students estimate what the last person would say if we counted around the circle by tens, many of them had more difficulty. But no one made far-out guesses, such as 1,000, and no one made an estimate of 30 or less. We counted by tens one time around the circle, and the last person landed on 200 (because we were counting by tens and there were twenty people). Then we counted again, this time by fives, and we landed on 100. We went around one more time counting by fives, and the last person landed on 200 again. "I wonder why Mishal landed on 200 again," I pondered aloud. Students got talking! There was so much buzz about this idea that I knew we could not have a whole-group discussion about it right away. I had to have them "turn and talk" (see Box 4.4) so *everyone* could get their own ideas out before we had a whole-class discussion in which only one person at a time talked about what had happened.

Many noticed that you count quickly with tens, so we got to 200 by only going one time around, whereas we needed to go around twice when counting by fives. Someone added on to this idea, diving into the computation part of the problem by saying that the reason we had to go around twice with fives was because five is half of ten. This spurred even more conversation as the second graders explained their thinking to one another and tried to convince others of their ideas.

My purpose with this counting sequence was to help some of the struggling students with counting by fives and to help others with estimation skills, but the routine was also rich enough that we could have a discussion

Math Talk in the Classroom: The Turn-and-Talk

Rich math discussion among students is a key element in their mathematical development. Math talk is an essential part of all the routines presented in this book. A "turn-and-talk" is one way to get everyone talking about an idea. It gives students time to process a concept with a partner before trying to follow a discussion with the whole class. It also gives the teacher time to listen in on students' thinking and make a mental note of key ideas that students can share. Here are some ways to establish turn-and-talk as part of your daily classroom life:

- Teach knee-to-knee, eye-to-eye: Teach children how to turn so their bodies are facing one another (knee-to-knee) and how to look at one another (eye-to-eye) when they turn and talk to a partner.
- Teach active listening: Teach children to listen to what their partners say with the intention that they will need to repeat it. Teach students to look at their partners and think about what they are saying. Ask students to restate by asking: *Can you say what your partner just said in your own words?*
- Begin with simple discussions and gradually build in complex discussions.

Knee-to-Knee, Eye-to-Eye

about why the last person said 200 when we counted by tens and why she said 200 again when we counted around by fives twice. I hadn't planned it that way. Actually, I hadn't even noticed that this particular big idea would come out, because I was so focused on the counting and estimating objectives. Yet, the discussion about the relationships between five and ten and about the magnitude of five and ten were essential number sense big ideas.

As you and your students establish the Count Around the Circle routine and begin playing with a variety of counting sequences, your own spontaneous discussions will arise. When you do Count Around the Circle daily with your students, you, the teacher, will also become better at planning the sequences based on your class's strengths and needs and better at watching for those big mathematical ideas to come up.

CHORAL COUNTING

Choral counting is simply counting aloud a number sequence as a whole class. One of the greatest benefits of this routine is that children hear and participate in the counting sequence without being put on the spot. Choral Counting is a routine you can use if the majority of your class is learning a new counting sequence (e.g., learning to count by twos for the first time) or is struggling with a particular counting sequence. Use the number grid or number line (or ten-frames with smaller amounts) as students are counting to help them see and use the patterns. Using the number grid or number line to help with the visual part of learning the sequences is a great support for students, but also remember to do Choral Counting without the visual supports so students rely solely on their memory of the sequence. This will help facilitate the application of the sequence to mental math and more efficient problem-solving strategies later on. To initiate higher-level thinking and discussion about patterns and relationships, frequently ask, "What do you notice about this pattern?" Box 4.5 offers ideas for getting started with Choral Counting.

Be sure to use Choral Counting in combination with Count Around the Circle when needed. I have watched students count incorrectly when the whole group is counting. They are whole-heartedly participating and enjoying the numbers, but they don't realize they are counting incorrectly! The risk here is that they will continue to count incorrectly, and then you will have to undo what they learned in error. I have seen this situation especially with students who are learning English and who are counting the teen numbers and decade numbers (as discussed in Box 3.4). "Sixteen" sounds awfully close to "sixty." If you notice incorrect counting during Choral Counting, try a Count Around the Circle so that the children can hear each number clearly. Or split the class into two groups and have one group listen while the other group counts, then switch. Just be sure that they are saying and hearing the correct sequence.

Getting Started with Choral Counting

You can differentiate Choral Counting much like you differentiate Count Around the Circle. In addition, try the following ideas.

Kinesthetic: Moving with counting helps some students internalize the counting sequence.
- When choral counting by ones, have children move a cube into their pile each time they count. This reinforces one-to-one correspondence and children can watch an amount grow. Eventually, have them make sticks of ten cubes. So, after the students say, "Ten," they start a new stick, after they say, "Twenty," they start a new stick, and so on.
- When choral counting by tens, have students show all ten fingers as you say each number. They clench their fists, and then when you say each number they stretch the fingers out to show all ten at once. This reinforces the idea that they are adding another ten with each number.
- When choral counting by ones, emphasize different groupings by doing different whole-body movements.
  o Count one through ten doing jumping jacks, then count eleven through twenty doing squats, then count twenty-one through thirty doing twists, and so on.
- Choral count steps to and from various places in the classroom. Be sure to estimate before starting! You might also have students do this individually. One-to-one can be tricky with this activity; emphasize counting slowly and walking slowly.

Small groups: Choral Counting is a quick routine that you can do with a small group prior to a guided math lesson or small-group activity. You can really individualize it in the smaller setting.

Moving back and forth between Choral Counting and Count Around the Circle will build more confidence with counting sequences. Both of these counting routines, and the combination of the two, get students thinking and talking about number patterns and number relationships. Children's continuous interactions with counting patterns and place-value ideas facilitate a deeper understanding of how the number system works. This understanding of numbers leads to efficient computational problem solving.

START AND STOP COUNTING

Start and Stop Counting is a routine that can be done as a Count Around the Circle, as Choral Counting, or by individual students. In Start and Stop Counting, students count up from a starting number and stop when they reach a predetermined point. For example, you can ask the class (or individuals) to count by tens starting with 26 and stopping at 176. This routine helps students remember a starting number and a stopping number in their heads while counting. It also helps young students learn to apply their newly learned counting sequences at various starting and ending points. The Start and Stop Counting routine also highlights differences between numbers. Using number line and number grid models with Start and Stop Counting will further draw attention to the differences between numbers and will help improve students' visual understandings of differences between numbers, problem-solving strategies, and mental math.

Michelle Gale, a kindergarten teacher at Bailey's Elementary, most often uses Start and Stop Counting in small guided math groups as a warm-up before the children begin solving the day's story problem. One winter morning, Michelle and I ran a lesson for a small group of three kindergarten students while her other students were working in math stations. As Michelle wrote 35 in black on a whiteboard, she told Samia that her starting number for counting was thirty-five. She then told Samia that she should stop at fifty-five, and wrote 55 in red and circled it. Samia started with thirty-five and counted by ones to fifty-five. She stumbled a bit at the decades (thirty-nine . . . forty and forty-nine . . . fifty), but with some wait time got it on her own. Then it was Jennifer's turn. Michelle said and wrote the starting and stopping numbers for Jennifer. They went through this same process with Bella. As each of the three children took her turn with Start and Stop Counting, the other two children were actively listening and counting the sequence to themselves in their heads. Bella was actually physically moving her head, but not saying anything aloud, as her two friends counted. It was a quick warm-up, the kids enjoyed their own personal challenge, and they benefited from listening to and encouraging one another. Michelle plans each child's starting and stopping numbers based on their individual counting abilities as well as the abilities of the other students in the group.

At the beginning of the school year, a group of my third graders were solid with counting backward by ones from twenty, but got lost if they started at a larger number, like eighty-six. I met with these students once a week for a month in a small group. Our warm-up prior to the small-group problem solving always involved Start and Stop Counting, with a focus on counting backward.

During one warm-up, they started at seventy-two and stopped at fifty. At the time, our whole-group lessons and their math stations involved working with money and making change. One of my students in this small group, Alex, made a connection to the making-change problems and said, "That made me think about seventy-two cents and giving money away until I had fifty cents." Alex recognized the idea of difference between two numbers. He created a separate problem (72 – ___ = 50) about unknown change in his head as he was counting. We took Alex's idea and looked at it more closely. We counted again, but I wrote 72¢ and 50¢ on the board since our context was money. I wrote the numbers in one horizontal line while the students counted (72¢, 71¢, 70¢, 69¢, 68¢ . . .). Students used the written notation to discuss Alex's understanding of the difference between seventy-two cents and fifty cents.

A couple of students really needed the visual to understand the relationship that Alex brought to light. One student, Blanca, saw two jumps of ten on the number line (from 72¢ to 52¢) then two jumps of one (from 52¢ to 50¢). She said that we could count backward by tens twice, then count by ones, and that would be quicker (see Figure 4.6).

Marjorie said, "You can also count forward by tens twice, then by ones. See, go from fifty and count sixty, seventy, then seventy-one, seventy-two.

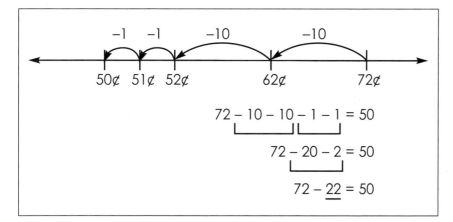

Figure 4.6
Blanca's Strategy

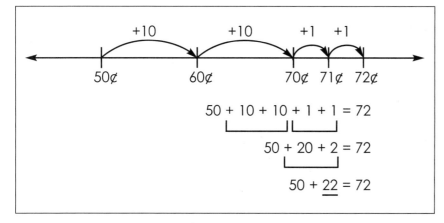

Figure 4.7
Marjorie's Strategy

It's the same thing!" She was exploring the idea that 72 − 22 = 50 was the same thing as 50 + 20 + 2 = 72, and was using a counting up strategy to solve the difference between 72 and 50 (see Figure 4.7).

I was not expecting those kinds of understandings to come out that particular morning, but we took it and ran with it. I saw a fantastic opportunity to develop their thinking through a discussion about their problem solving with Alex's money problem. I made the instructional decision to capitalize on their developing understanding of the important concept of "difference" and did my planned lesson on another day.

I also used Start and Stop Counting as a whole-class routine often throughout the year as my third-grade students learned about larger numbers (up to 999,999) and the place-value patterns involved in becoming proficient with counting, naming, and writing numbers greater than 1,000. We would start and stop at numbers like 3,092 and 3,116 to help them with that tricky leap from 3,099 to 3,100. So many times they wanted to count to the next thousand (for instance, they often said, "3,099," then said, "4,000"). At times I told the children that we would start with a number like 1,089 and stop at 2,000. I would hope that someone would complain and say, "That will take too long!" If so, they had to prove why it would take too long. If no one

Getting Started with Start and Stop Counting

Sequences to start with (counting by ones):
- Start at twelve and stop at eighteen (practice counting on from those tricky teens).
- Start at fifty-seven and stop at seventy-two (practice getting over the decades).
- Start at forty-three and stop at eighty-three (maybe someone will notice that you counted four tens or that the difference between forty-three and eighty-three is forty).

Sequences that keep students flexible with counting on and counting back:
- Start at twelve and stop at eighteen, then start at eighteen and stop at twelve.
- Start at fifty-seven and stop at seventy-two, then start at seventy-two and stop at fifty-seven.
- Count leaps of ten going forward and backward.

Sequences to help students gain an understanding of fractions and decimals and larger numbers:
- Start at $4\frac{1}{2}$ and count by halves (or fourths), stopping at 14.
- Start at 9.0 and count by tenths using decimals (9.0, 9.1, 9.2, 9.3), stopping at 10.5.
- Start at 12.25 and count by 0.25 (or 0.5), stopping at 13.75.
- Start at 1,095 and count by ones (or fives or tens), stopping at 1,110.
- Start at 12,992 and count by ones, stopping at 13,012.

Ask questions to facilitate discussion about patterns, such as odd/even patterns:
- *If you start counting at twenty-five and count only by fives, what numbers could you stop at?*
  - This question gets your students thinking about factors of twenty-five and multiples of five.
- *If you count by twos and start with 1,222, what numbers could you stop at?*
  - As students grapple with the idea that the numbers have to be even, ask them to prove it and if it will always be true: *Why would the number need to be even? Will it be even if we keep going into the millions?*

Ask questions that help students think about magnitude and the difference between numbers:
- *If you count by ones starting at 12 and stopping at 112, will it take you a long time to count or not much time to count? What if you start at 12 and stop at 20?*
- *If you count by ones starting at ten and stopping at fifty, will it take you a long time to count or not much time to count? What if you count by tens starting at ten and stopping at fifty?*
  - Here the difference between ten and fifty remains constant, but the time it takes changes—that's a really interesting idea to explore and it helps students think about how quick and efficient it is to use leaps of ten.

said anything, we would start the count and they eventually figured out that we were going to get tired of counting long before we got to 2,000.

A variety of ideas can come out of Start and Stop Counting as students discuss the relationships among numbers, visualize the big idea of difference between numbers, and learn more about the structure and patterns of the number system. Box 4.6 outlines some ideas discussed in this section about Start and Stop Counting, but there is much more you can do. Use these ideas as a place to start your planning, but get creative! Listen keenly to your students to find out what they already know and what their confusions are with place value, numbers, counting sequences, and differences between numbers. Plan Start and Stop Counting based on your students' current understandings and based on their challenges and/or misconceptions.

USING COUNTING ROUTINES IN THE SMALL GROUP

Mary Anne Buckley and Christy Hermann, two kindergarten/first-grade multiage teachers, use Math Boxes during math workshop (much like children's beloved Book Boxes, which contain several books selected for each child based on the child's reading level and needs), and, in particular, during daily routines. Their students have the following items in their Math Boxes:

- Number grids (0–30, 0–100, or 0–280, depending on students' needs)
  - Black number grids
  - Number grids with colors that highlight the patterns
  - A blank number grid for writing in the numbers
- Number cards (with pictorial representations) or numeral cards (just the written symbol)
  - The cards often have just the numeral, although some of the cards have a ten-frame/dot representation or a base ten blocks representation to give the student a visual representation of the amount. The decision about which to use depends on each student's needs.
  - Cards for 1–30
  - Teen number cards (10, 11, 12, 13, 14, 15, 16, 17, 18, 19, 20)
  - Cards for decades (10, 20, 30, 40, 50, 60, 70, 80, 90, 100, 110, 120)
- A Ten Wand (ten Unifix cubes, with five of one color and five of a different color) for the visual image routine
- Water soluble markers for writing and erasing on the number grids
  (See Appendix B for a blank ten-frame, dot cards with teen numbers, and number grids.)

Mary Anne's and Christy's students bring their Math Boxes with them when it's time for small guided math groups or when their teachers pull together a group with similar needs. The Math Boxes are full of tools to lend a hand with numeracy routines. Mary Anne and Christy have students use something in the box for a quick five minutes or less as their warm-up to the work they will do in that small math group. Their students use the boxes in independent math stations, too. The children often come to math share time with new understandings because of peer conversations they had while working with the materials in their Math Boxes.

In addition to using Math Box materials for counting routines, Mary Anne and Christy have students use the materials for practicing a variety of skills. These two teachers use the number grids for the counting routines or to practice writing the numbers they are counting. The number cards are used in many different ways. One way to use them is to have the students mix up the cards and then sequence them from least to greatest or greatest to least. The number cards are also used for quick identification, much like flash cards. They can also be used for a quick game of "Which Is More?" or "Which Is Less?" (Some people call the game "War," and we also call it "Top-It," a term from *Everyday Mathematics* [University of Chicago School Mathematics Project 2007].) They use the dot cards and ten-frames for identifying amounts, but also for developing part-whole relationship understandings. For example, in addition to asking, "How many?" they also ask, "How many are missing?" or, "How many more to make a five?" or, "How many more do you need to make a ten?"

Mary Anne and Christy use these Math Box tools with small groups, in addition to other whole-class mathematics routines, as a way to differentiate the needs of their learners. Using routines in this way helps them to assess their students continuously and to individualize instruction on a day-to-day basis. It can be overwhelming to differentiate lessons for a wide range of learners, but routines are one small component to your math workshop. If differentiation for your entire math block feels daunting, differentiating for your number sense routines is one way to start. And, using routines in this way is a very responsive way to plan your instruction based on students' strengths and needs.

ORGANIC NUMBER LINE

The Organic Number Line routine helps second- and third-grade students develop a mental linear model for fractions and decimals. (See Box 4.7 for definitions of models used in fractions work.) The Organic Number Line is one section of a "whole number" number line; with it, you magnify the number line from 0 to 2 (see Figure 4.8). It is "organic" because your students

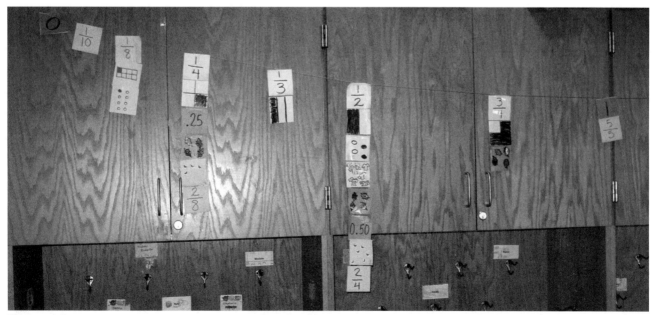

Figure 4.8
An Organic Number Line from My Third-Grade Class

continuously add to it throughout the year. It is ever changing based on the experiences in your class.

To create the Organic Number Line in my third-grade class, we used a string that was six feet long and cards labeled with numerals and pictures. I introduced the number line by placing the card with the numeral 0 on one end and asking a student to put the card with the numeral 1 anywhere on the number line. Lizbeth volunteered, and placed the 1 fairly close to the 0.

"If Lizbeth put 1 there, where does the $\frac{1}{2}$ go and how do you know it goes there?" I asked. Adib took the $\frac{1}{2}$ card, placed it halfway between the 0 and the 1, and explained that he estimated that this point was about halfway between 0 and 1. Next, I moved the 1 and asked, "Where does the $\frac{1}{2}$ go now?" The children could answer the question by identifying the new point, and could explain how they knew where $\frac{1}{2}$ went.

"So, why do those points move?" I asked. This question spurred a discussion about the concept of the whole. The children talked about how the whole changes depending on where the 0 and 1 are located. I explained, "You identified the $\frac{1}{2}$ easily no matter where I put the 0 and 1. That means that the $\frac{1}{2}$ is your benchmark. You can find out where other fractions lie on the number line by using that benchmark."

During this initial discussion, other children added $\frac{1}{4}$, $\frac{1}{8}$, $\frac{3}{4}$, $\frac{1}{3}$, $\frac{2}{4}$, $\frac{4}{8}$, $\frac{15}{16}$, and $\frac{1}{100}$ using the benchmark $\frac{1}{2}$ or using their knowledge about the relationships among halves, fourths, and eighths. They were able to add these points to the Organic Number Line because they had had many experiences with these fractional amounts through problem solving before we began this routine. They had solved many story problems about sharing pizzas, brownies, and pies ("fair share"), made fraction bars out of paper (a lesson from Marilyn Burns [2001]), and played with set models, such as, "What fraction of this group of students is boys?" They had had concrete experiences with many fractional amounts and had developed visual models of these amounts in their heads. Now they were ordering these symbolic numbers on a number line based on their concrete and visual experiences with fractions.

Students require strong visual understandings of fractions prior to embarking on the Organic Number Line routine. Without a mental image of what $\frac{1}{2}$ or $\frac{3}{4}$ looks like, an understanding of what $\frac{1}{4}$ of a pie means, or an understanding of the idea that fraction and decimal numbers are part of a whole amount, students will struggle with understanding this linear model. Children need a variety and plethora of experiences with "fair share" story problems. They need visual understandings of region models of fractional amounts (like pies, brownies, and pizzas) and set models of fractional amounts (like the fraction of crayons that are blue) as well as clear mental models of important benchmarks, like halves, thirds, and fourths.

In our third-grade classroom, we had a special place for the Organic Number Line, where it was displayed and evolved throughout the year. We

BOX 4.7 **Definitions of Visual Models for Work with Fractions**

Linear model: A number line or ruler model on which fractions are often represented by fraction bars or fraction strips or on the ruler.

Region model (or area model): Whole amounts such as pies, pizzas, and cookies, often represented by pattern blocks or geoboards, on which fractions are represented as segments of the whole. (For example, "This is one-quarter of the pie.")

Set model: Individual, distinct objects (e.g., counters, chips, toys, or people) that are grouped together to demonstrate a fractional amount. (For example, "Three out of four people are wearing red.")

usually sat in a circle during our whole-class routines to better facilitate a class discussion; however, we had special meetings for our Organic Number Line routine and gathered in a "clump" (group) in front of it. Sometimes I led the discussion. In these cases, I held up a card that showed either a picture of a fractional amount or a written numeral representing an amount, and I asked the students where they thought the card belonged on the Organic Number Line. Other times, various students (sometimes the whole class if we were doing a longer warm-up) had cards and decided individually or as a whole group where their cards belonged and why.

It is best to start your discussions of the Organic Number Line with the half and whole benchmarks:

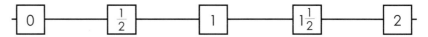

Then, think of ways that halves and wholes are represented, and add to your number line:

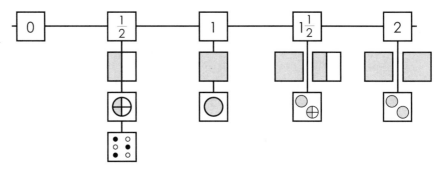

Later, add the quarter benchmarks:

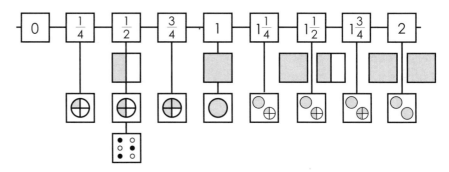

After these initial benchmarks are established, hold discussions on subsequent days about where $\frac{1}{3}$ is located on the number line. Ask students, *How did you figure that out?* and *How was your thinking different from finding the $\frac{1}{2}$ point?* Discuss how they know where $\frac{1}{8}$ and $\frac{1}{16}$ are located and how their strategies for finding these points changed.

Interesting discussions take place after this initial introduction. In this particular routine, guide your class to set up the structure of the number line using common benchmarks, then plan which cards you will use to highlight specific mathematical ideas. Here are some examples of big ideas in fractions that you can teach and questions you can discuss using the Organic Number Line:

Big Idea: Benchmark and Counting Sequences
- *Where does this number go on our number line? How do you know?*
- *What numbers can you think of that go between $\frac{1}{2}$ and 1? How do you know that number goes between these two benchmarks?*

Big Idea: Equivalency
- *You said that $\frac{2}{4}$ goes here with $\frac{1}{2}$. Prove that $\frac{2}{4}$ and $\frac{1}{2}$ are equivalent.*

Big Idea: The Whole and Parts of a Whole
- *Why does $\frac{1}{2}$ go here and $1\frac{1}{2}$ go over here?*
- *Are this half and this half the same amount?* (Show two models representing $\frac{1}{2}$, each with a different whole.) *Prove it!*

Big Idea: Linear Model as a Tool
- *What on the number line helped you figure that out?*

Big Idea: Region and Set Models
- *Here we represent $\frac{1}{2}$ with this picture:*

Can you think of another way to show that number? (Students might show $\frac{1}{2}$ as a set model by showing 4 yellow leaves out of 8 leaves total or show $\frac{1}{2}$ as a region model represented with a pizza cut into sixteenths, with 8 pieces gone.)

Big Idea: Doubling and Halving
- *What is half of that amount? Where does that fraction go on the number line?*
- *How did you know that $\frac{2}{4}$ goes in the same spot at $\frac{1}{2}$?*
- *How did you know that $\frac{1}{8}$ should be halfway between $\frac{1}{4}$ and 0?*

As I plan for discussions around these big ideas, I also think carefully about which cards to use—both the amount and the representation (symbolic or pictorial). If I know that my students have a visual model in their heads for halves, fourths, eighths, and thirds, I'll use a symbolic notation:

$$\boxed{\frac{1}{2}} \quad \boxed{\frac{3}{4}} \quad \boxed{\frac{4}{8}} \quad \boxed{\frac{1}{3}}$$

If some students are struggling with knowing where $\frac{2}{8}$ goes, I'll use a picture of a region model (here, showing $\frac{2}{8}$ of a rectangular pan of brownies):

I use stickers to make cards that show set models (here, two of the four leaves are yellow, which is equivalent to a half, so this card goes at the point on the number line that represents $\frac{1}{2}$).

Twp out of four leaves are yellow.
Half of the leaves are yellow.

Planning these routines based on students' concrete and visual experiences and knowledge will help them better understand fractions as a linear model—fractions on a number line. The Organic Number Line is another excellent model (in addition to visual region/area and set models) to help students develop a fuller understanding of fractional ideas. Some of the benefits of using this routine include the following:

- *Stronger linear and measurement understandings of fractions.* In the past, I often observed that my students could recognize and compare fractions like $\frac{1}{4}$ and $\frac{1}{8}$ and discuss the idea that $\frac{1}{8}$ is less than $\frac{1}{4}$, but they struggled with using fractions when measuring. For example, when they used a ruler or counted by a fractional amount, they often were stumped by $\frac{1}{8}$ being smaller than $\frac{1}{4}$. After working with the Organic Number Line, they were better able to apply what they knew about $\frac{1}{8}$ and $\frac{1}{4}$ because they understood both what that quantity looked like (as a region model) and where it fit in a sequence in a linear model. The Organic Number Line helped them make connections between their visual understanding of fractions and the linear, measurement quality of fractions.
- *Increased skill and flexibility when counting with fractions.* Students often referred to the Organic Number Line when we counted by fractional amounts during Count Around the Circle. The model helped them see the "jumps" as they counted, such as when we counted by eighths:

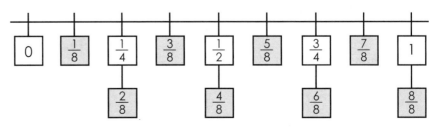

- *Deeper and broader understanding of equivalent fractions.* Counting by fractional amounts, like eighths, combined with the linear model of the number line as a visual, helped my students develop an understanding of equivalent fractions. They were better able to recognize that $\frac{1}{2}$ is the same as $\frac{4}{8}$, $\frac{2}{4}$, and $\frac{5}{10}$ and that all fractions have multiple names or are represented in multiple ways.

- *Increased ability in estimation with fractions and better understanding of relationships among fractions.* Students were more apt to recognize that $\frac{1}{8}$ is closer to 0 than it is to 1 and that $\frac{7}{8}$ is closer to 1 than it is to 0. Students referred to the Organic Number Line to prove their estimates, citing the distance between fractions and the relationships among fractions.

- *Increased ability to use benchmarks to compare fractional amounts.* Once we started using the Organic Number Line, students were more easily able to use benchmarks like $\frac{1}{2}$ and $\frac{1}{4}$ to compare fractions without the support of a visual.

- *More exact measurements in math and science.* While using the Organic Number Line, I noticed that my third graders were using fractions to be more exact in their measurements during science. For example, we measured winter wheat over several months, and as we worked with the Organic Number Line during our number sense routines, their abilities to use exact measurements improved greatly. They were applying their sense of fractional amounts and their understanding of the linear model to a variety of measurement problems during science discussions and in their observational drawings and notes (see Figure 4.9).

Early foundations in understanding and visualizing fractional amounts are essential for developing complex ideas later. Children need to be able to understand part-whole relationships, relationships among fractions, relationships among fractions and decimals, comparisons of fractions to the whole amount, and equivalency. The linear model especially supports children in seeing the patterns in counting by fractions, which helps them gain more solid understandings of the relationships among fractions and relationships between a rational number (fraction/decimal) and a whole number. The Organic Number Line is one more component in helping students develop these concepts throughout the year. Use Count Around the Circle or Choral Counting while using the Organic Number Line as a reference, then facilitate discussions about the positions of numbers and their relationships on the Organic Number Line. Keep it organic and keep it growing.

• • •

Counting routines help students learn sequences and understand where numbers fall in the number line and in relation to one another. Students not only learn how to count but also build understandings of how the base ten, place-value number system works. They gain insight into relationships

Figure 4.9
Marjorie measures winter wheat using fractions.

among numbers. They see patterns in the number system that lead them to develop efficient strategies in problem solving. These concept and skill developments are key foundations to students' sense of number. In addition, counting routines are a playful way to experiment with quantities and test out ideas. Enjoy the spontaneous discussions that come out of these routines and lead to deeper understandings. The children will surprise you!

5

PLAYING WITH QUANTITIES

Making Sense of Numbers and Relationships

What is the value of the 1 in 21,732? The 1 no longer means one object. Its value is 1,000. With that idea in mind, think about the value of the 1 in the following numbers:

0.01 (one tenth of a tenth, or one hundredth, or 1 ÷ 100, or ten thousandths, or 10 × 0.001)

0.1 (one tenth, or 1 ÷ 10, or ten hundredths, or 10 × 0.01)

1 (one)

10 (one ten, or ten ones, or 10 × 1)

100 (ten tens, or 10 × 10)

1,000 (ten hundreds, or 10 × 100)

10,000 (ten thousands, or 10 × 10 × 10 × 10, or 10 × 1,000)

100,000 (ten ten-thousands, or 10 × 10 × 10 × 10 × 10, or 10 × 10,000)

The eighteenth-century European mathematician Pierre-Simon Laplace expressed admiration of the beauty of the base ten, place-value number system:

> *It is India that gave us the ingenious method of expressing all numbers by means of ten symbols, each symbol receiving a value of position as well as an absolute value; a profound and important idea which appears so simple to us now that we ignore its true merit. But its very simplicity and the great ease which it has lent to computations put our arithmetic in the first rank of useful inventions.* (quoted in Eves 1988, 135)

When I really stop to think about the functionality and elegance of our number system, I am in awe of the remarkable way humans figured out how to organize, symbolize, and name quantities. It was quite a feat to invent a system for keeping track of large amounts and conveying relationships among quantities. The development of the base ten place-value number system took centuries. Place-value ideas are difficult for young children to grapple with; as teachers, it is important to keep in mind that humans grappled with the big ideas of unitizing and place value for hundreds and hundreds of years.

The base ten numeration system and the concept of place value are crucial components of students' number sense development. Therefore, it is essential that students understand the number ten and play with groupings of ten. Messing around with ten and powers of ten will help children understand ten as the base of our number system. Also, students must regularly play with numbers to understand place value and the role of the position of a digit within a number. The routines in this chapter provide you with ideas for playful ways to experiment with numbers and explore these important place-value concepts.

Place value (a positional number system) keeps track of amounts and organizes large quantities. It is truly a neat and orderly arrangement, although not simple to learn. The idea that a numeral can take on different values depending on its position in a number is an organized and efficient way of keeping track of amounts and organizing quantities. For example, the numeral 6 can mean six ones (as in the numbers 6 and 456), six tens (as in the numbers 60 and 5,761), or six millions (as in 6,000,000 or 26,000,000). The numeral's value is dependent on its place in the number.

When students understand the way numbers work in our base ten number system, the way they look at and use numbers changes. Numbers become a lot easier to work with. Students begin to use more efficient strategies, which usually involve breaking apart numbers (decomposing) and putting them back together (composing). For example, when given a problem like 52 + 47, instead of starting with 52 and counting up, students who understand place value are more likely to think about the numbers in terms of 50 and 2 plus 40 and 7 and use the tens and ones to solve the problem. They either use jumps of ten or add the tens together to make 90, then add the ones together to make 9, thereby recomposing the number to make 99.

BOX 5.1 WHAT'S THE MATH?

The Base Ten Number System and Place-Value Concepts

Our base ten number system (also called the decimal system or the Hindu-Arabic system) uses ten different numerals (also called digits), or symbols, to represent abstract quantities: 0 through 9. Verbal and written expressions of numbers demonstrate the basic principle of this system—grouping units into tens. Think about the number 32. The written expression signifies that there are three groups of ten and two ones: $32 = (3 \times 10) + (2 \times 1)$. The number words (verbal expression), such as *thirty-two*, also denote groupings of tens and ones (in this case, *thirty* means three tens and *two* means two ones).

In addition, the base ten number system is a positional system; the numerals take on different meanings depending on their place in the number. The numeral 9 means nine in the number 209. The numeral 9 means nine hundreds in the number 972. This is a difficult concept for young children. They are required to change their thinking about what the word and symbol *nine* means depending on the context: Is it nine individual things or is it nine groups?

Groupings of ten and the position of numerals work together in this system. Each digit in a number expresses powers of ten. For example, in the number 7,219, each digit increases by a power of ten as you move to the left. The first place value means nine (nine units). The second place value means one ten (1×10). The third place value means two hundreds (2×100, or $2 \times 10 \times 10$). The fourth place value means seven thousands ($7 \times 1,000$, or $7 \times 10 \times 10 \times 10$). In expanded notation, 7,219 is expressed as $7,000 + 200 + 10 + 9$. In terms of powers of ten, the quantity is expressed as $(7 \times 10^3) + (2 \times 10^2) + (1 \times 10) + (9 \times 10^0)$.

Keep in mind that the primary purpose of the routines in this chapter is to encourage students to play with quantities, breaking them apart and putting them back together, as well as think about how numbers are composed and how the base ten place-value system works (see Box 5.1). As we'll see, place value and understanding the base ten number system are essential building blocks of students' number sense and their ability to think arithmetically and algebraically.

THE TEN WAND

I have used the Ten Wand routine to help young children think about how numbers (in particular, the number ten) are composed. During my years as a math resource teacher, I visited my kindergarten and first-grade classrooms every tenth day of school dressed up as the Queen of Ten (a long-standing tradition at Bailey's Elementary that predates my tenure as the Queen of Ten). During several of these visits I brought my Queen of Ten Wand, which was made of five green Unifix cubes and five blue Unifix cubes. The tricky thing about this wand was that it broke easily, and this was compounded by the fact that the Queen of Ten was very clumsy. Each time the wand broke, we would see what the wand broke into (5 and 5, 6 and 4, 7 and 3, 8 and 2, 9 and 1, and of course, the turnaround facts 4 and 6, etc.). The children found it miraculous that there were always ten cubes when we put the wand back together.

The drama of the Queen of Ten worked to get students enthusiastic about playing around with the special number ten. The real number sense understandings came out as teachers used the idea of the Ten Wand and turned it

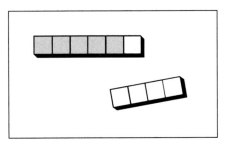

Figure 5.1
Charlie's Broken Ten Wand

into a number sense routine. Students built their own wands and teachers kept a set of wands in their classrooms. As students played with and broke the Ten Wand, teachers engaged the children in a discussion of the mathematics.

"Oh, no! Charlie's wand broke again!" exclaimed Ms. Buckley one day (see Figure 5.1). "How many on the floor and how many in his hand?"

"There's four on the floor," said Sindy.

"How do you know that's four?" asked Ms. Buckley.

"I see the two and two," said Sindy.

But John was not so sure and counted by ones to check it. "One, two, three, four. Yeah, there's four," he said.

"There are six in your hand—see the five blue ones and the green one? That is six," Yasmin explained. Ms. Buckley asked her to repeat that and show everyone what she meant.

"So if you put the four green ones back on, you will have ten again," said Carlos. He came up front, picked up the four green cubes from the floor, and reattached them to the wand.

Ms. Buckley rephrased what Carlos had said to reinforce it: "So, Carlos, you are saying that six and four make ten?"

"Yep," Carlos confirmed.

Recording discussions like these on chart paper and engaging in similar discussions over a couple of weeks initially, then periodically throughout the year, will help students make sense of combinations of ten (the wand helps with the mental image of what composes ten), part-part-whole relationships, and the commutative property ($6 + 4 = 4 + 6$), and will solidify their ability to use the five- and ten-structures in solving problems. Box 5.2 further explains the mathematics of this routine.

In particular, the Ten Wand routine is a playful way for students to become automatic with the combinations of amounts that total ten. Knowing these combinations is an essential building block to success with the base ten place-value system later on. Since our number system is based on ten, computation will be much easier if students are fluid with combinations of ten. For example, when solving $27 + 36$, creating a "friendly ten" by applying knowledge of combinations for ten creates a more accessible problem. The 7 ones in 27 need 3 more ones to get to the next ten (take 3 ones from 36 and give them to 27), allowing the student to work with $30 + 33$, numbers much more conducive to mental math.

After solving the problem $124 + 386$ in his head, my third-grade student Anthony explained to the other students, "I'm always trying to find a way to make ten to make [the problem] easier. I guess that's why ten is so important. It helps me do it in my head." He showed his peers that this problem was easier because the numbers in the ones and tens already made a ten. Anthony explained how he solved $124 + 386$: "Twenty and 80 make 100. Four and 6 make 10. So, 100 plus 300 plus 100 (from the 80 plus 20) equals 500, plus there's a 10 from the 4 plus 6, so the sum is 510."

WHAT'S THE MATH?

The Ten Wand and the Wonderful Number Ten

The Ten Wand routine is both a visual and a kinesthetic way for students to understand the number ten, learn ways to compose and decompose ten, and learn about properties of numbers. The following text explains the mathematics concepts behind the wonderful number ten and the Ten Wand routine:

Combinations of Ten

- The more students see and work with combinations of ten, such as 6 + 4, the more they become automatic with the visual quantities and these facts.
- Fluency with combinations of ten helps students use efficient strategies in computation later on. Students who are comfortable with composing and decomposing ten are more likely to apply this skill to use the closest ten ("friendly ten" or "bridge to ten"), make jumps of ten, or use a tens and ones strategy.
- A deeper understanding of ten helps students' understanding of place-value relationships later on.

Part-Part-Whole Relationships

- The ten is the whole when one part of the Ten Wand breaks off. To support this understanding, ask students: *How many do you still have? How many are on the floor? If we put it back together, how many now?*

Commutative Property

- As you use the Ten Wand routine, students will inevitably engage in conversations about commutativity. The visual image of five green cubes and five blue cubes helps children see that, for example, 6 + 4 is the same as 4 + 6. It's easier to see six cubes when there are five green and one blue than it would be if all six cubes were the same color.

Using the Five- and Ten-Structure

- The five green cubes and five blue cubes (or five each of any two colors) on the wand help students use the five-structure (quinary) to help them conceptually subitize amounts.

Students who are comfortable with composing and decomposing ten are more likely to use their understandings to use the closest ten ("friendly ten" or "bridge to ten"), make jumps of ten, or use a tens and ones strategy in computation later on. Being fluent with ten is crucial for success in using the base ten system, and the Ten Wand routine is one way to build this fluency.

WAYS TO MAKE A NUMBER

The routine that I call Ways to Make a Number is also called by a variety of other names, such as Name Collection Boxes (from *Everyday Mathematics* [University of Chicago School Mathematics Project 2007]), Today's Target (from *Number SENSE* [McIntosh et al. 1997a and b]), and Number of the Day (which I've heard used by various teachers). The essence of Ways to Make a Number is that it supports students in thinking about numbers in flexible ways by having them think about how the target number is composed and how it can be decomposed. If the target number is ten, students might write *5 + 5, 7 + 3, 12 – 2*, draw ten dots, and so on. The work samples on pages 84 to 90 show variations in how children think about Ways to Make a Number.

During the beginning stages of this routine, it is important to leave the routine open-ended to see what students come up with on their own. As you get to know how students are thinking and see patterns in their work and discussions, you can begin to add constraints to Ways to Make a Number. For example, as students become proficient with making addition combinations of ten, instead of just saying, "Write as many ways to make ten as you can think of," now you can say, "Write ways to make ten with three addends," or "Think of ways to make ten using subtraction."

For teachers, the difficult part of this routine is knowing what to look for in students' work in Ways to Make a Number and knowing how to highlight important math concepts during the discussion of the routine. Here are some common big ideas to look for:

- Decomposing the number into expanded notation

$$470$$
$$400 + 70 + 0$$

- Various groupings of ones, tens, hundreds, and thousands

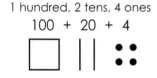

1 hundred, 2 tens, 4 ones
100 + 20 + 4

12 tens and 4 ones
120 + 4

1 hundred, 1 ten, 14 ones
100 + 10 + 14

- Using a pattern (see Figure 5.2)

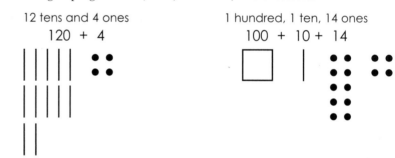

$$49 + 1 = 50$$
$$48 + 2 = 50$$
$$47 + 3 = 50$$
$$46 + 4 = 50$$
$$45 + 5 = 50$$

Figure 5.2
Using a Pattern for Ways to Make 50

- Interesting ways of thinking about numbers using coins, pictures, subtraction, tallies, multiplication, and so on (see Figure 5.3)
- Highlighting a wide variety of ways of thinking about a number (See Figures 5.4a, b, c, and d for ways various students made 100.)

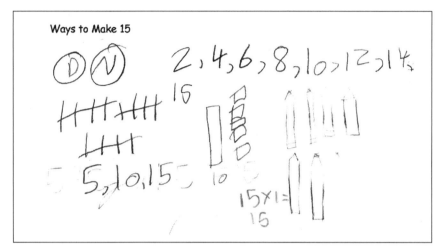

Figure 5.3
Interesting Ways of Thinking About 15

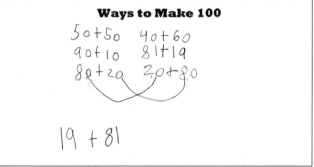

Figure 5.4a
Catie highlights using the commutative property, then uses compensation.

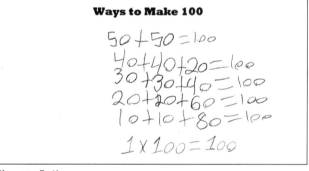

Figure 5.4b
Luis highlights using three addends.

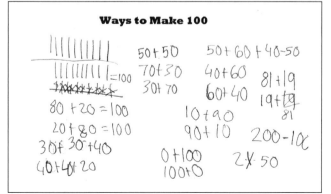

Figure 5.4c
Lisa highlights combining with 50, then taking out 50.

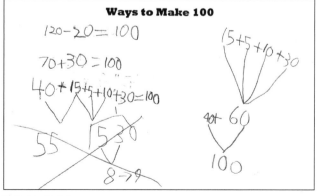

Figure 5.4d
Randy highlights decomposing a number into many smaller amounts.

As you and your students do the Ways to Make a Number routine on a regular basis, you will become more familiar with what math concepts and skills to highlight, and students will become more creative and will begin to take more risks. You'll also start to see that different numbers bring about different kinds of discussions. You will want to choose numbers that hit on the big ideas your students need to explore or numbers that will scaffold their success in other problem-solving activities scheduled for your math block.

Here is a classroom vignette that demonstrates the discussions and learning that grow out of Ways to Make a Number. My second-grade students were busy writing all the ways they could think of to make 102. This was our third day using this routine as our warm-up to math workshop. The day before students had done Ways to Make 15 and Ways to Make 42, because those numbers were in their story problems for math workshop that day. On this day my purpose was to have a discussion about a three-digit number. I was hoping students would look closely at groupings within 100 and I was curious about what they'd do with the 2. My secondary goal was for them to listen closely to one another during our discussion and to apply some new ideas the next day. To spell out this goal I explained, "As we talk about 102 today, listen closely to your friends' ideas and think about ways they made 102 that you didn't think about. We are going to use the same number tomorrow—we'll do Ways to Make 102 again—and you can try out their ideas tomorrow."

During the discussion it became apparent that students were looking closely at groupings within 100. Many of them thought about the ways to make 100 and just added 2 to that amount. One of Ashley's ideas was a little different from these three-addend equations. She thought of a way to make 100 (50 + 50), then added the 2 to one of those numbers to get 52 + 50. Her description of how she thought of 52 + 50 sparked a connection with Gavin.

Gavin said, "I thought about it the same way you did, Ashley. I did 40 plus 62 because I knew 40 plus 60 makes 100. It's kind of like Wesley's over there. He did 40 plus 60 plus 2, and I just put the 2 with the 60 for 40 plus 62."

Another student made 102 with the equation $10 \times 10 + 2$. Many students didn't understand the equation and weren't convinced that this was one way to make 102, mainly because the multiplication symbol and the addition symbol were both there. Also, multiplication was a fairly new concept for many of them, and they needed to "see" what 10×10 meant.

After two minutes of turn-and-talk, during which partners shared ideas about how the equation might work, Rosa shared that one of her ways of making 102 could explain it. "I like to count to the number like I did here . . . 10, 20, 30, 40, 50, 60, 70, 80, 90, 100 . . . and then I did 101 and 102. The 10 times 10 part is like counting my tens." (She counted her groups of tens out loud.) "See? There's ten groups of ten."

"That's how Alex and I thought about it," said Michelle, referring to her discussion with her turn-and-talk partner, "but we drew base ten blocks.

There's ten sticks and two ones, so it's like ten groups of ten and two ones. If you put all the sticks together it makes a flat like that one." She pointed to Alex's drawing of a square (representing a hundreds flat) and two tiny squares (representing two ones). Michelle's connection between these pictorial models helped many students "see" what $10 \times 10 + 2$ (a symbolic notation of an abstract idea) meant. These moves from concrete understandings to pictorial understandings, then finally to abstract understandings, are critical in students' number sense development. The Ways to Make a Number routine provided these students with an opportunity to share ideas and help each other make important connections among various representations of a number.

Michelle was hitting on a big place-value idea, so I broke in and asked, "Does anyone know what Michelle means?"

Kevin jumped in right away to restate Michelle's explanation and pointed to the pictorial representation of base ten blocks on the board. "The ten sticks and two cubes means the same thing as the ten tens and two," he said. "You can trade the ten tens for 100."

Michelle added on, "The picture with the ten tens helps me see the ten times ten plus two. I think I get it better now." Michelle's statement helped me see that she was on the frontier of an abstract understanding. It was apparent that her visual model, combined with the class discussion, helped her make this leap to an abstract understanding of the composition of 102.

As we wrapped up the discussion, I gave students a minute to reflect on what we had discussed that day, which of the ideas were a new way of thinking for them, and which idea they thought they'd try out the next day.

As promised, we did Ways to Make 102 again the next day. We continued to build on the previous day's discussion, particularly about the way 100 can be one group of 100 or ten groups of 10. More students tried some addition equations with two addends instead of three (such as $32 + 70$). Someone even tried a division problem, which extended our discussions about groupings even more. Anthony said that 306 divided by 3 equaled 102. He showed his thinking with three boxes, with 102 in each box. He explained, "First I thought of 102 plus 102 plus 102, and that was easy to add. I just added the hundreds to make 300 and the ones to make 6. Then I went backward—306 divided into three groups is 102 in each one."

Ways to Make a Number provides students with opportunities to play around with quantities, think about how quantities are composed, try different ways to decompose quantities, and experiment with relationships within a quantity. When children do Ways to Make a Number, they bump into the big ideas embedded in place value and grouping. Discussions about the ways students have grouped tens together and ones together help them think about base ten and powers of ten. Conversations about the values of different digits within a number bring up ideas about the position of a numeral and the different meanings it takes on in different places within a

BOX
5.3
Questions and Statements for Today's Number

When is _____ big?
When is _____ small?
When is _____ a lot?
When is _____ very little?
Make _____ using three addends.
Make _____ by subtracting two numbers.
Divide _____ in half.
Double _____.
Divide _____ into four equal parts.
What other ways do you think about _____?
What is _____'s relationship to ten? Is it more than ten or less than ten? By how much?
What is _____'s relationship to the age of your mom? (Other relationship comparisons include your age, the age of your grandpa, the height of our winter wheat, your weight, the number of times you've been to Six Flags, and other number situations found in daily life.)
If today's number is _____, how much is one group of _____?
How much is ten groups of _____? (This question could be explored with concrete materials to help students see the amount ten times.)

number. Students will move amounts around within a quantity and more fully understand how quantities are composed of different groupings. And, as students play with these groupings and the patterns in numbers, they'll learn about compensation strategies. Each student thinks about a quantity differently, so providing time for them to discuss their thinking with one another will broaden everyone's perception and understanding of the quantity.

TODAY'S NUMBER

The Today's Number routine helps students expand their thinking about any given number in relation to different situations and scenarios. In this routine, you pick a number—let's say twelve—and ask a variety of questions about it: *When is twelve big? When is twelve small? When is twelve a lot? When is twelve very little?* (See Box 5.3 for more question and statement ideas.) The number twelve holds different meanings in different contexts. The Today's Number discussions you have with your students will guide them to think about relationships among numbers depending on what the number is describing in the world.

To initiate discussion about Today's Number in my class, I write questions or statements on sticks (I use tongue depressors or popsicle sticks) and have one student at a time draw one of the sticks and read the question or statement aloud. Other students give a silent thumbs-up if they have an idea in response to the question or statement. For the question *When is twelve a lot?* students often say things like, "Twelve pizzas is a lot of pizza," or "Twelve minutes of running in place is a lot." For the question *When is twelve very little?* the children come up with ideas such as "Twelve grains of sand is not much sand" or "Twelve seconds of running in place is not very much." Some questions or statements ask students to compose or decompose Today's Number, much like they do in Ways to Make a Number. For instance, to make twelve using three addends, students write statements like $10 + 1 + 1$, $4 + 4 + 4$, and $5 + 5 + 2$. We write all ideas on the board so we can see that the number means different things in different situations. (Figure 5.5 shows our notes for the number 14.)

Today's Number and Stories

To extend the Today's Number routine, I often have students come up with stories to match the equations they write in response to statements like *Make twelve using three addends.* This helps students think about when twelve might be broken up in a particular way. For example, the equation $10 + 1 + 1$ might prompt a story about "one more":

> A girl had 10 beads. Her string was almost full so she took one more bead. She realized she could still fit one more on the string. Now it's full and there are 12 beads total.

Figure 5.5
Luis shows Today's Number is 14.

The equation 4 + 4 + 4 could prompt a story about "evenness," or equal groups:

> A boy is making a pattern out of three different colors. He needs 4 orange beads, 4 red beads, and 4 brown beads. He needs 12 beads in all for his necklace pattern.

These contexts and conversations about twelve are playful, and they build students' sense of number beyond counting a set of objects. The written symbol *12* and the word *twelve* are human inventions for discussing an abstraction. But, what does twelve mean beyond just the counting of a set of twelve bears? Today's Number will assist you and your students in exploring that question. Play around with Today's Number and see what happens. It will reveal a lot about your students' understanding of the quantity. The authors of *Adding It Up* point out that "although normally taken for granted, it is remarkable . . . that any number . . . can be used in so many ways. That versatility helps explain why number is so fundamental in describing the world" (National Research Council 2001, 71).

Relating Today's Number to 10 and 100

Another piece to explore with this routine is Today's Number's relationship to 10 and 100. You can prompt discussions about these relationships by asking questions like these: *If Today's Number is twenty-two, is it more or less than ten? By how much, and how did you figure it out? How far away is 22 from 100? How do you know?* Some students may need to use concrete materials or see a number line or a number grid to visualize a number's distance from 10 and 100.

It's interesting to see how students use 10 and 100 as benchmarks to find the differences between numbers. For example, as shown in Figure 5.6, Luis figured out how far away 22 was from 100 by ignoring the 2 in the ones place, using what he knew about 10 to figure out that 80 was the difference between 20 and 100, and then subtracting 2 from 80 to get 78. Melanie, on the other hand, used what she knew about 10 to figure out she needed 8 more to get to the next ten. The next ten was 30, so she then used what she knew about 10 again to realize that there were 70 jumps (or 7 jumps of 10) to get to 100. So, she concluded, 22 is 78 away from 100. Talking about these relationships to 10 and 100 will facilitate a deeper understanding of the magnitude of numbers. Calculating differences or seeing differences (using visuals or concrete objects) between a number and 10 or 100 will help students use benchmarks of 10 and 100 in other problem situations.

For younger students, comparing amounts to ten will help them understand those tricky teen numbers and will guide their understandings as they explore larger two-digit numbers. Use questions like these to prompt their thinking: *Is Today's Number more or less than ten? How much more?* Pulling out

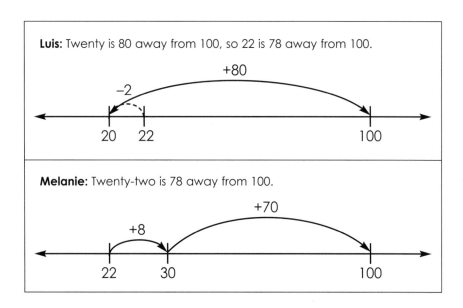

Figure 5.6
Luis's and Melanie's Work with 22

students' Ten Wands will help them see that twelve is just two more than ten. I recommend using sticks of cubes (like the Ten Wands) or the base ten blocks as visual and concrete tools while students explore numbers' relationships to 10 and 100.

Relating Today's Number to the Multiplicative Place-Value System

Repeated groups of tens, hundreds, thousands, and so on make up the place-value system. This is because it is a multiplicative system. As you move to the left of a number, each place is multiplied by ten, and as you move to the right of the number, each place is divided by ten. Playing with grouping ideas is another way to establish understandings of the base ten, place-value system. Use Today's Number and play with one group of that amount versus ten groups of that amount. What happens? Let's use twenty-two again. One group of twenty-two is twenty-two. Ten groups of 22 is 220. A hundred groups of 22 is 2,200. It is very effective to use base ten blocks to watch this amount multiply. The concrete materials facilitate exploration and understanding as the multiplicative patterns are discovered.

Whether the Today's Number routine leads to discussions of a number's meaning in various contexts, the ways a number can be composed or decomposed, a number's relationship to 10 and 100, or down another avenue, this routine helps students build number sense. Give your students the opportunity to play with Today's Number, and watch their math creativity flourish.

MENTAL MATH ROUTINES

Sometimes students just need a prompt to rely on themselves to do math mentally. The mental math routines do just that. Moreover, you may be surprised to find that your students use more efficient strategies when they unravel a problem in their heads rather than on paper. As their teacher, you will find out some interesting things about their thinking when you prompt them to explain "what your brain did." Cathy Seeley, NCTM president from 2004 to 2006, wrote about mental math in the *NCTM News Bulletin*:

> *Mental math need not depend on rote memorization. In fact, the development of mental models for numbers and operations is greatly facilitated by students engaging in purposeful experiences with concrete objects and number patterns. Teachers play a vital role in making sure that these experiences are connected in meaningful ways to the mathematics we ask students to learn.* (2005)

To institute mental math routines, it is best for students to sit in a circle where they can more easily talk to one another. Explain that the objective of this routine is to help students solve problems in their heads. Discuss the expectation that students will share their strategies so that everyone can learn efficient strategies and/or new ways of thinking from each other. Distinguish that sometimes it is better to solve a problem with paper and pencil, sometimes it is helpful to solve it with tools, and sometimes it is more efficient (or necessary) to solve a problem in your head (i.e., do mental math). You can present the students with a problem in a variety of ways: tell a story problem, show and read a story problem, or write an equation on the board (just numbers, no story). Provide wait time so students have time to think through the problem on their own (use the silent thumbs-up to help you manage the wait time). Once everyone or most students have had an opportunity to think through the problem on their own, ask several students to share their thinking either verbally (as you write what they say on the board) or visually by writing their own thinking on the board while explaining how they did in it their heads. Either way, make sure you have a space for students to sit near a whiteboard or chalkboard with lots of blank space. This is critical because you need space where you can write students' thinking as they verbalize their strategies (or where they write down their own strategies). This makes their thinking visible to others. The math may make sense in their heads as they are explaining it out loud, but their peers may have difficulty following an individual's thought process without a written thought map on the board.

When students solve a problem in their heads, they usually use what they know about place value, relationships among numbers, patterns, and visual images to figure it out. Our job is to help them make explicit what is going on in their heads. Asking questions like, *What did your brain just do to figure it out?* or *What did you see in your head when you solved it so quickly?* helps students realize their understandings. At the same time, students' mental math explanations provide you with a door to their thought processes and with an opportunity for ongoing informal assessment.

Be careful as you write a student's thinking on the board. Check in with the student to make sure you are representing his or her thinking accurately. Sometimes you will need to restate and say, "So are you . . . ?" or "Let me make sure I understand what you are doing. Does this [what you wrote on the board] show what you did in your head?" Ask other students if they can restate their classmate's thinking: "Can someone explain what Luz did in her head?" Give students the opportunity to restate their thinking if it is not clear. It can be quite tricky to try to explain what your brain is doing, especially if you solved a problem quickly and efficiently and then are asked to break the process into steps or segments. It takes some practice to be able to verbalize the thought process of mental math. This is one routine that requires patience, especially if students are not used to stopping, really thinking through what they did, and then explaining their thinking in such a way that the other children understand how they solved a problem.

To plan the mental math routines, use your ongoing informal assessments to understand where your students are in their use of strategies. Choose numbers and problems that will facilitate discussions about relationships among numbers, place-value ideas, and grouping ideas. With kindergarten students and first-grade students, it is important to use a context. Use story problems about the students in the class or about you. For example, if you want students to think about a part-part-whole situation and you want to encourage a discussion about combinations of ten, you could create a story like this:

I have 10 apples. 8 apples are green and the rest of my apples are red. How many red apples do I have?

With second- and third-grade students (and older first-grade students), try some problems without a context. Tell your students that you will present an equation for them to try to solve in their heads without paper or tools. Write out the problem symbolically, such as 32 + 24 = ? Sometimes, use a story or a context, but other times just present a problem using numbers and symbols (an equation) for students to work with mentally. See if there are differences in the ways they solve the problems.

As with the other routines, plan the mental math routines based on what students are able to do and almost able to do. Your ongoing informal assessments will be your ally in planning these routines. Andy, a second grader, helped me do this with his class. Andy was solving the following problem during math workshop:

Samia has 2 packages of pencils.
Each package has 12 pencils.
How many pencils does Samia have?

My ongoing informal assessments about Andy's mathematical thinking told me that he was beginning to gain a strong sense of place value. During the Ways to Make a Number routine, he broke two-digit numbers into tens and ones and discussed groups of ten. He would prove his solutions with the base ten blocks or with cubes grouped in tens. When counting, he was able to tell me that thirty-four is ten more than twenty-four. So, when he was working on the problem about Samia's pencils, I was surprised to see him drawing a line for each pencil, one by one. I knelt down next him and asked, "So, what are you thinking?"

Andy replied, "Well, Samia has two boxes of pencils and in our classroom those boxes come with twelve pencils. There's two twelves."

He understood the problem type and knew how to solve it, but I still wondered why he was drawing each pencil when I knew he had a strong emerging sense of place value and groupings of ten. So I dug a bit deeper: "So, what's your estimate? How many pencils do you think she has?"

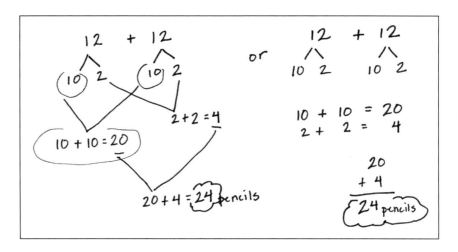

Figure 5.7
Andy's Strategy: Two Ways to Represent His Mental Math

"I know she has twenty-four," responded Andy.

"How do you know?" I asked.

"Well, twelve is a ten and two, so there are two tens and two twos. Two tens makes twenty and two twos is four so she has twenty-four pencils," Andy said confidently.

"Let me write down what you just did in your head," I said, trying to keep up with Andy's words (see Figure 5.7).

"Is this what you did, Andy?" I asked, referring to the diagram on the left in Figure 5.7.

"Yeah, because there's two tens and two twos," he said.

"So which one of these shows exactly what your brain did?" I asked, pointing to my representation of his mental math and then pointing to his lines for each pencil. By comparing his original drawing of each pencil with his mental math work as represented in my diagram (Figure 5.7), I tried to get him to see that he does not need to laboriously draw out every pencil.

"That one," he said, pointing to my representation of his mental math, "because I said it to you really fast," he replied.

I realized that Andy's one-by-one drawing of each pencil did not represent what he actually did in his head. He just didn't know how else he could represent his thinking. There were other students in the class who drew the pencils out one by one because it was the only way they knew to "show their thinking." So, their teacher and I planned a series of mental math routines to help build their confidence in solving the problems in their heads as well as figuring out ways to record exactly what they did in their heads. We chose numbers similar to those in the problem about Samia, as we knew many of the students could easily decompose numbers like those (small two-digit numbers) in these problems: 10 + 17, 24 + 12, and 15 + 15. We also chose problems that would facilitate a discussion about counting by tens and/or using tens and ones to solve problems with larger numbers: 36 + 10, 36 + 20, and 36 + 30. Finally, we tried some counting up and counting back problems:

99 + 3, (or 99 + 1 if 99 + 3 proved too difficult), 64 – 5, 2 + 58, 2 + 79, and 78 – 10.

Number choice is a challenge for teachers for this routine. You need to choose numbers that are accessible to everyone, but still challenging. You also need to choose numbers that are fun to play around with. In addition, you often have a specific teaching objective and need to choose numbers that highlight efficient strategies and/or important place-value ideas. See Box 5.4 for ideas for where to begin. As always, watch and listen carefully to what your students do and how they are thinking about the numbers. Play with the problems yourself before presenting them to the children. The more you and your students work on the mental math routines, the easier they become to plan and the more interesting the discussions become.

 BOX 5.4

Number Choice for Mental Math Routines

The following numbers were selected to encourage use of specific strategies. Remember, these strategies are not the "right" ways or the only methods for solving problems. Be open and listen to the strategies children construct and use. Sometimes you might use numbers to encourage a specific strategy, but students may come up with a way to solve the problem that is just as efficient or more efficient! With the following suggestions, I have also included ways to record students' thinking as they talk out their strategies. Always check with the students to be sure you're representing their thinking accurately. For example, ask, "Does this picture show what you did in your head?" Have students draw or restate if your drawing does not represent their thinking.

Making Ten

- Kindergarten and first-grade children might start to make connections to their hands. They might "see" that 6 + 4 = 10 in their heads, but prove that 6 + 4 = 10 by showing it on their fingers.

    6 + 4 "I had six rocks. Sacha gave me four more. How many do I have now?"

    1 + 9 "Quinn only had one rock. At recess he found nine more. How many does he have now?"

- As students become more fluent with tens, try problems in the teens or twenties and use numbers that involve the combining of ones to make a new ten (regrouping).

    16 + 4

    5 + 15

    12 + 8

    22 + 8

    29 + 1

    29 + 11

Counting On or Counting Back

- A large number paired with a small number encourages students to quickly count up from, for example, 99 by ones (99 . . . 100, 101, 102). If a student explains this mental math strategy, you can show the student's thinking on an open number line.

    99 + 3

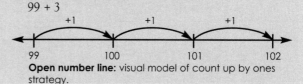

    Open number line: visual model of count up by ones strategy.

    99 + 1

- Here, a large number paired with a small number again encourages students to count on; however, this time the larger number is second. See if students begin with the larger amount. If someone does, have that child explain his or her thinking about why he or she started with the larger amount and then counted up. For the problem 2 + 58, some students might also quickly see the 8 and 2 as a ten and add 10 to 50 to make 60.

    2 + 58

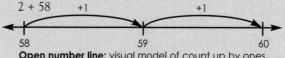

    Open number line: visual model of count up by ones.

    2 + 58
    Students might also quickly recognize that the 8 and 2 make a ten and add that 10 to 50 to get 60.

    50 + 10 = 60

    2 + 79

(continued)

BOX 5.4   **Number Choice for Mental Math Routines** (*continued*)

- Again, here a larger number paired with a smaller number encourages counting back. For 78 – 10, you can watch for students counting backward by ten or by ones.

64 – 5

78 – 10

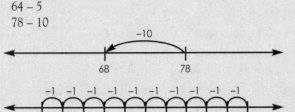

Open number line: Students might count back by ten or by ones.

Decomposing Numbers into Tens and Ones

- The following problems are usually easy to work with, so students can focus on the tens.

10 + 17

24 + 12

Students think of the 24 as a 20 and a 4 and the 12 as a 10 and a 2. Then they add the tens together, then the ones. Finally, they put the tens and ones together.

$$24 + 12$$
$$20 \quad 4 \qquad 10 \quad 2$$
$$20 + 10 = 30 \text{ and } 4 + 2 = 6$$
$$30 + 6 = 36$$

15 + 15

36 + 10

36 + 20

With these numbers students might decompose the numbers and use a tens and ones strategy or think about the tens and count up/make jumps of ten.

$$36 + 20$$
$$30 \quad 6 \qquad 20$$
$$30 + 20 = 50$$
Add the 6 back on:
$$50 + 6 = 56$$

or

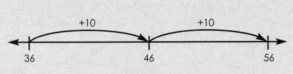

Sometimes these numbers also provide students an opportunity to make jumps of ten. It just depends on the way students think about it. Both the tens and ones strategy and the jumping by tens strategies are solid, efficient strategies.

Using Ten or Compensation Strategies

- These problems encourage using the "friendly" ten, either by adding/taking away amounts or by compensation.

9 + 11

Students recognize that 9 is one away from 10 and 10 is easier to work with. Then they will either (1) combine the numbers and take the extra one off or (2) take one away from the 11 (because they added one to the 9), then combine the amounts.

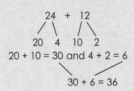

Using Ten
9 + 11

+1 ↓

10 + 11 = 21
I added one to 9 so now I need to take it off.
21 – 1 = 20

Compensation
9 + 11
+1 ↙ ↘ –1
10 + 10 = 20

11 + 19

21 + 29

19 + 27

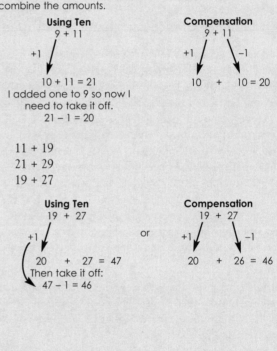

Using Ten
19 + 27

+1 ↓
20 + 27 = 47
Then take it off:
47 – 1 = 46

or

Compensation
19 + 27
+1 ↙ ↘ –1
20 + 26 = 46

I used mental math routines to help my third-grade students develop stronger subtraction strategies as well as get in the habit of thinking through what they knew about numbers prior to diving into a problem. In the beginning of the year, I noticed that a few students used the traditional algorithm for 100 – 92, which works, but I wasn't sure if they realized how close 92 was to 100. I used a mental math routine during a two-week period to find out.

On the first day of the routine, I started by writing the equation 100 – 92 on the board, and waited for most of the class to show a silent thumbs-up. Not surprisingly, many students simply counted up and arrived at the correct answer of 8. By taking away the paper and pencil and urging students to do it in their heads, many students solved it accurately and efficiently. Some of these students who counted up and got 8 previously did it incorrectly with paper and pencil, trying to use the traditional algorithm. I used the routine to help them make the link to what they had done with paper and pencil. So, once we discussed different strategies for solving 100 – 92 and there was consent that 100 – 92 = 8, I said, "It's interesting that we came to a consensus, because last week, many people would have disagreed. These were answers that came up last week: 8, 92, and 118." I wrote the equations and answers on the board (see Figure 5.8). Pointing to the equations on the board, I asked, "Which answer is correct?" Now students had to prove that 8 was correct and examine the reasons why 92 and 118 came up as answers the previous week.

The following day, the mental math problems I posed included 52 – 48 and 52 – 12. When students mentally solved 52 – 48, most counted up from 48 (49, 50, 51, 52) and said that 4 was the answer. For the problem 52 – 12, many students agreed with their classmate who said, "Ten less than 50 is 40,

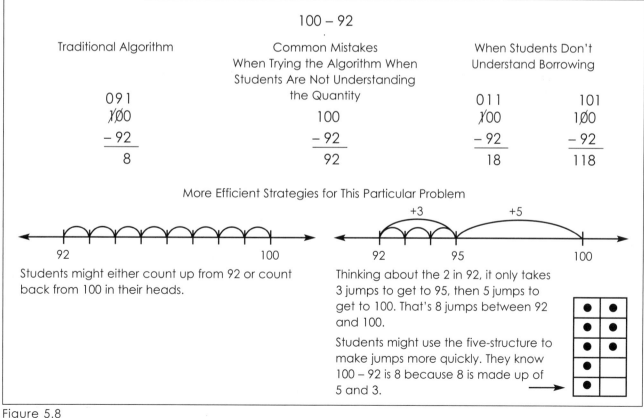

Figure 5.8
Strategies and Common Mistakes When Solving 100 – 92

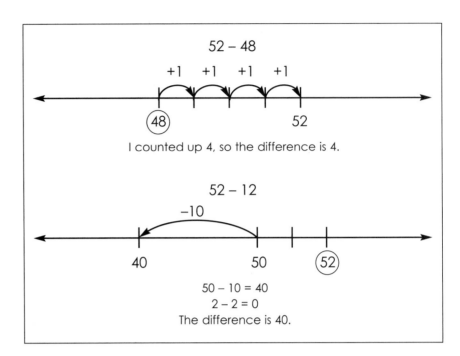

Figure 5.9
Choosing a Subtraction Strategy Based on the Numbers in the Problem

and 2 minus 2 is 0, so it's 40." (As the student spoke, I wrote *50 – 10 = 40* and *2 – 2 = 0* on the board.) We were then able to compare the two problems and analyze why so many people counted up for the first problem, but took amounts off for the second problem. "They are both subtraction problems," I said. "Why did so many of you count up on the first problem and take off amounts on the second problem?" This led students into a discussion about using different strategies depending on the numbers. In the first problem, 52 – 48, the number 48 is close to the number 52, so it is easier to just count up. In the second problem, 12 is far from 52, and the 10 and 2 are easy numbers to work with and take off from 52 (see Figure 5.9).

Mental math routines provide opportunities for students to reflect on their mathematical thinking. I often ask students, *What do you do when you don't have tools in front of you? If it's too tricky to solve without tools or paper and pencil, what's your estimate? Why did you use this strategy instead of that strategy?* These questions help students rely on the mental strategies they know, whether the strategies are visual understandings of quantities, mental number lines, or use of their fingers to keep track of amounts. Their understandings as well as their misconceptions about our base ten place-value system will be highlighted as they explain their mental math strategies. Conversations surrounding these big ideas about how numbers work will emerge. With mental math routines, students think about their thinking, and they employ and/or grapple with place value and grouping concepts naturally. These are key factors in the development of your students' number sense.

● ● ●

The Ten Wand, Ways to Make a Number, Today's Number, and mental math routines are occasions to play with quantities and build understandings about place value and the multiplicative base ten system. As the teacher and facilitator, remember that these are difficult ideas for your students to tackle and that understandings of how quantities are related and how we represent their relationships will take time to develop. It took humans centuries to figure it out! Base ten place-value ideas are challenging, but that is part of the fun and enjoyment of mathematics. Wrestle with the ideas, allow your students time to play around with numbers, and provide lots of experiences and probing questions so that students will bump into the key ideas that are the foundation of how we represent quantities.

6

CALENDAR AND DATA ROUTINES

Using Numbers Every Day

During calendar time, children learn about organizational systems that they will use throughout their daily lives. In elementary school, students learn about the cycles of the seasons, months of the year, days of the week, and daily activities in the school day's agenda. Calendar time is a wonderful way to bring the class together and explore these systems and cycles that organize our lives.

Calendar time and data routines provide authentic times to use number sense. Frequently, as classes discuss the calendar or data they have collected, the focus of the discussion is not on the mathematics. The mathematics is embedded *in* the discussion—it is being applied and used authentically within a context. Discourse is at the heart of calendar time. It is a time for children to talk about what they see, clarify their thinking, share their unique strategies, and develop understanding over time. As you read about calendar and data routines in this chapter, think about how numerically literate students apply their number sense in these settings and ways that you can deepen discussions about number sense in your current calendar and data routines.

Calendar Routine Prompts and Questions

BOX 6.1

You know where your students are in their learning. Ask the right questions for the right students—try to give them a question on their level or a question that will advance their thinking. You can differentiate questions, numbers, and/or scenarios.

Basic Recall Prompts and Questions

- Ask a student to read today's date.
- Ask a student to count the days in this month.
- Read an important date for the calendar, and have a student find the date and write the event or celebration on the calendar.
- Try asking the following questions during calendar time:

    If March ends on a Monday, what day of the week will April begin on? What about May?

    How many days until _____?

    How many weeks (or months) until your birthday (or other exciting days)? (This question will assuredly spark debate!)

    Is it three or four days until your birthday? (Should you count today or not?)

    If Monday is March 17th, what day of the week will it be on the 20th?

Prompts and Questions to Use During an End-of-Month Ceremony

- *Find the 9.*
- *Find the number that is made of a ten and two.*
- *Find the number that represents this amount. (Show a card with 5 dots.)*
- *Find the number one less than 7.*
- *Find the number one more than 10.*

More Open-Ended:

- *Find a number greater than 5.*
- *Find a number less than 15.*
- *Find a number close to 10.*
- *What patterns do you notice? How does that help us? Does it make sense?*

USING THE CALENDAR TO BUILD AND USE NUMBER SENSE

At the end of every month, Emelie Parker's kindergarten students ceremoniously took the numbers off their school calendar. After singing a song about the months of the year and counting to thirty on the November calendar, her students removed the numbers on the calendar through a series of differentiated questions. Emelie asked Maritza, who was working on numeral identification, to find the 9 and take it off the calendar; she asked Ethan, who was working on teen numbers, to find the number that had a ten and a two (12). She asked Adrian and Mary, who were working on comparing amounts and numbers, to find a number less than 15 or a number greater than 9 and take it off the calendar. Emelie thought about a question that would help each student successfully apply a skill or concept that they were currently working on. Once all the numbers were taken down, the students said "good-bye" to November and "hello" to December. To recompose the new month, the students thought about what day of the week it was and where they'd put the 1 the next day, the first day of December. Emelie and the students would then let the month of December unfold by adding a number to the calendar each day and would look at ways to make that number (you can make four with two twos or with a three and one) or practice counting the days that had passed during the month. Very young children may need to "see" the number of days represented by Unifix cubes, because the numeral 4 might not mean much to them yet. One option is to have one color of Unifix cubes available so trains of the quantity can be built and then broken apart to show the parts of the number. That way, students see how much 1 is and how much 2 is and how much 3 is. (Box 6.1 lists ideas for prompts and questions to use during calendar time.)

• • •

During our first Math Collaborative session at Bailey's Elementary, Mary Anne Buckley, a first-grade teacher, said, "I don't like calendar time. I know my students need to know the months of the year and the days of the week, but it feels so inauthentic." She said that she was thinking about not putting up her "cute" calendar this year and was wondering what to do instead. Another teacher prodded her for more information, saying, "But calendar time is a time for students to understand the cycles of the seasons and the months. They need to understand how to use the calendar—it is a life skill."

Mary Anne was struggling with the authenticity of her classroom calendar. Her "cute" calendar was the premade calendar she bought at the teacher store. It was a rectangular grid of seven squares by five squares that came with thirty apples for September, thirty-one pumpkins for October, and so on. She didn't like how static this calendar was—you couldn't see the preceding month or subsequent month, because you took down the numbers each month and put up new numbers for the new month. She reflected on how she used her own calendar and datebook constantly, looking ahead at dates and going back to previous dates. She felt that the problem with her school calendar was that it was one large flat sheet that didn't allow for referring to earlier or later months. Her students were not seeing how each month's numbers were connected. They were not using the calendar in the relevant way that Mary Anne used a calendar in her own daily life. Mary Anne uses her calendar with a purpose; students should use a calendar in a similar fashion.

As the other Math Collaborative teachers listened to Mary Anne talk this out, they got into a discussion about taking apart an entire calendar and fitting it together like a puzzle. When you recompose the calendar in this way, you can see that if August ends on a Saturday, then of course September begins on a Sunday. You can see the patterns more clearly. Of course, you wouldn't want to do this with every class of students, especially very young children who are learning what numerals symbolize, but this discussion helped the teachers think more clearly about their purposes for calendar time and how they used the calendar in their classrooms.

Following this discussion, Mary Anne decided to buy a large desktop calendar at an office supply store. She posted two or three months at a time so students could see how the months were connected, go back in time to remember dates and events that had passed, and look ahead to future dates. Through the discussion with her colleagues, Mary Anne's purpose for calendar time became clear—to explore the bigger concept of the passage of time with her students. The mathematics (recognizing numbers, counting days, exploring one more/one less, solving comparison problems, and so on) is embedded within the discussions around the concept of the passage of time. Numbers, counting, and patterns organize the way we think and talk about the passage of time.

Other teachers in that Math Collaborative session decided to keep their premade, store-bought, school calendars because they saw value in the number sense activities they did with the school calendar. Even so, Mary Anne's concerns influenced their thinking. Many of the teachers hung a twelve-month calendar next to the premade calendar. They marked important days (birthdays, field trips, etc.) with their students at the beginning of each month on the twelve-month calendar, while doing other number sense activities with the premade school calendar. One teacher hung an additional calendar in the kitchen play area for the children to use in their imaginary play.

Mary Anne found that the use of the twelve-month calendar led students to ask more questions and solve problems like: *How many days until Ms. Buckley's birthday? How many months until our next field trip?* and *When did we go to the museum? I want to write the date in my story.* These questions revolved around the passage of time and the children needed to use numbers and operations to find the answers. When the new year came along, students said good-bye to their old 2010 calendar and welcomed their new 2011 calendar and again went through the process of writing in important days and special events for the coming months.

CALENDAR ROUTINES AND COLLECTING DATA OVER A LONG PERIOD OF TIME

Common calendar routines for the primary grades include stating a complete sentence saying the day of the week, month, day, and year (*Today is Friday, September 5, 2008*); counting the days in the month; looking for patterns (with questions such as *What will tomorrow be?* and *What date will it be on Friday?*); and so on. Many teachers also use this opportunity to say a sentence in the past, present, and future (*Today we are . . . , Yesterday we . . . , Tomorrow we will . . .*); sing songs about the days of the week or months of the year; and integrate other content areas into the calendar routine (for example, social studies, by discussing holidays and historic days).

In addition to working with the calendar in these commonly used ways, calendar time is also an excellent opportunity to collect Earth cycles data for long-term use. For instance, students can collect weather data, temperature data, and sunrise and sunset data. These data collection contexts provide plentiful opportunities to immerse students in number sense concepts.

Amy Henrickson, a kindergarten teacher, noticed that her students were often surprised when it was sunny and cold or cloudy and hot. Aware that her students would begin learning to read thermometers in first and second grade, she wanted to help her students differentiate early on between weather and temperature. To do this, I helped her set up two graphs to be a part of her morning calendar routine. She continued to use her premade picture graph that had several weather options: sunny, cloudy, rainy, windy, foggy, and snowy. Then, she and I made a temperature graph that included options for hot, warm, cool, and cold (Figure 6.1). Box 6.2 shares our thought process for designing the graph.

We re-created the weather graph every month. The temperature graph, on the other hand, was a permanent part of our long-term data collection. At

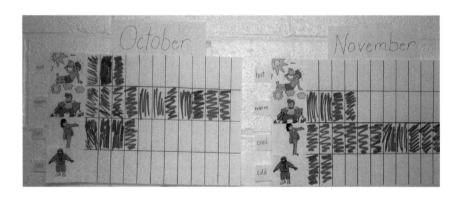

Figure 6.1
Temperature Graphs for Young Children

the end of each month, we posted the temperature graph along the top of the back wall so students could see our data change over time. Although this routine sharpened the kids' skills for recognizing temperature and differentiating weather and temperature, it was merely a routine for only that purpose in the first few months of school. It took time for the students to see the trends in the data. Collecting long-term data like this takes patience and persistence—wait for the students to begin seeing these patterns and trends.

That year, December was the month when our students started to recognize the temperature pattern and began talking about it. One day, after the Weather Wizard (a classroom job title) finished coloring in yet another cold day on the bar graph, Amal said, "Look, we have so many more cold days in December than we did in August." Amy and I latched onto that teachable moment, and the students took off on a discussion about the changing temperature from September to December. The number sense that students used involved number magnitude, comparing amounts, and estimation (which led to science predictions).

Evan made comparisons: "There were no cold days in September but there were three cold days in October."

Sadia used what she knew about magnitude: "Yeah, but that's still not very many."

"That's not very many, but there will be lots of cold days in January," Genesis predicted. "Maybe ten cold days."

Adrian also made a prediction, "I think it will be more than ten cold days."

Ella said, "It's going to get warmer in the spring." That comment took us off in another direction, talking about what the graph might look like in April. Their teacher, Amy, encouraged further predictions and asked, "How many warm days do you think we'll have in April?"

"Well, maybe there will only be three cold days and lots of warm days . . . so maybe twenty warm days," said Evan, again using his skill of comparing numbers and graphs.

We were able to use this long-term data throughout the year and had monthly conversations, which gradually grew more sophisticated, about temperature and seasonal cycles. In these discussions, students counted, used their sense of magnitude, estimated, used numbers to compare trends, thought about range, and read graphs, all of which developed their number sense.

Third graders can use this same routine in a different format. My third-grade students read the temperature daily and recorded it on a line graph. One student did this job at the end of every day (we rotated jobs every two to four weeks). Collecting this data over the course of the year led to varied mathematics conversations, the topics of which included understandings of range (for example, the temperatures during December ranged from 34 degrees Fahrenheit to 52 degrees Fahrenheit, which was a range of 18),

BOX 6.2

Teacher-to-Teacher: What's the Difference Between Warm and Cool?

Before our kindergartners arrived for their first day of school, Amy and I were busy envisioning what our math routines would look like. We discussed having the temperature graph and the weather graph separate and began designing the temperature graph. I proposed that we needed to have cold, warm, and hot on the graph. Amy said that warm can also mean hot. I argued that warm is not hot, but she countered with, "When I say, 'It's warm in here,' it really means it's hot."

"But warm is in between hot and cold. I'm not sweating on a warm day," I responded.

Amy said, "Well, what about 'cool' temperatures?"

We ended up giving it a rest for the day because we could not agree about what should be on the temperature graph. We spent time debating this and really thinking it through before settling on a graph that had cold (when you need a coat and gloves), cool (when you need a jacket), warm (when you do not need a jacket and you wear short-sleeved shirts), and hot (when you are sweating and want to wear shorts).

I provide this example because many readers might wonder what our thinking was behind this graph, and also to exemplify that teachers take time to really think through routines, play with the ideas and the math themselves before working on the ideas with children, and get into the deeper meaning of why we are doing what we are doing in our classrooms. Math talk among students is key; it's also important to have this kind of talk and reflection among teachers.

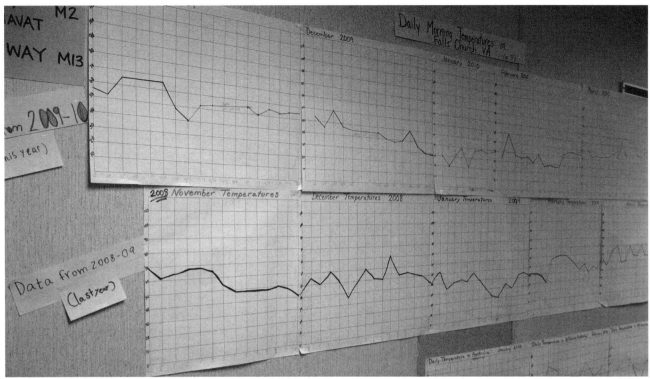

Figure 6.2
**Temperature Data Displayed on Line
Graphs Over a Long Period of Time**

benchmarks (80 degrees Fahrenheit feels hot, whereas 40 degrees Fahrenheit feels cold), and estimation ("It's probably about 70 degrees Fahrenheit today"). Students' sense of number was enhanced through conversations about temperature variations and through learning how to read the thermometer.

Embedded within these conversations about line graphs, trends, and data are science concepts that will lead your class to think more deeply about why the temperature changes and what happens to the Earth during different seasons. For example, our data displayed sudden drops and rises in temperature on specific days (Figure 6.2), but students pondered why it seemed to never be more than a 10-degree drop (in most cases in Virginia). Students were using number sense within a real-world context. Although the routines occur daily throughout the year, the use of their number sense is not routinized; rather it is contextualized and imbued with deep understanding and hands-on application.

The temperature routine naturally links with another data collection routine—recording sunrise and sunset data. My third-grade students used the U.S. Naval Observatory Web page "Complete Sun and Moon Data for One Day" (http://www.usno.navy.mil/USNO/astronomical-applications/data-services/rs-one-day-us) to find the local sunrise time and sunset time and recorded the times daily (this is also one of our classroom jobs) on a double bar graph (Figure 6.3). This routine further drives student conversations

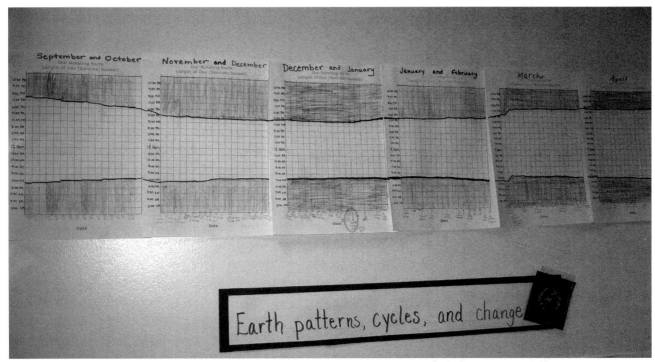

Figure 6.3
Sunrise and Sunset Data Displayed on Double Bar Graphs

about what happens to the Earth during different seasons and why the days get shorter in the fall and longer in the spring. The mathematics that emerges from these conversations tends to revolve around patterns and using number sense to predict what will happen next. With multiple experiences using the data and having conversations about the data, students also get a better sense of time and how time is organized.

In order for deeper discussions about the patterns, cycles, and trends within these data to emerge, the data need to be collected daily. Daily data collection can be managed in many different ways. In my classroom, we have a job for every student and rotate these jobs every two to four weeks. Five of our classroom jobs involve collecting data: Weather Monitor (records temperature), Daytime Tracker (records sunrise and sunset times), Moon Watcher (monitors the phases of the moon), Calendar Keeper (keeps track of the days in school—I will discuss this routine in the next section), and Data Supervisor (knows how to do each of the data jobs, fills in when needed, helps others record the information correctly, and/or checks that the data are correct). Although we collected data each day, we did not talk about the data daily. Discussions often came up spontaneously as students noticed patterns and trends. In addition, I created mini-lessons for science and math to discuss the data and use it as a springboard to talk about Earth cycles. I planned those mini-lessons at least monthly starting in December, when a sufficient amount of data had been collected. (See Box 6.3 for tips, ideas, and questions to use for data routines.)

Data Routine Tips, Ideas, and Questions
Assigning Data Collection Jobs

It is important to allow students some element of choice for their data collection jobs. However, for management purposes, in the beginning of the year I choose their jobs for them based on skill level and needs (they indicate first, second, and third choices, and I take their requests into account). This allows for differentiated instruction through pairings. Students who are comfortable reading the thermometer, sunrise/sunset data, and moon phases data and recording that information hold these jobs in the beginning of the year in order to get the routines going. During this time, the student I assign to be Data Assistant is often not as comfortable with these skills, but the job of Data Assistant gives him or her time to observe and learn how to do the other jobs and pushes his or her learning to an independent zone.

During the second quarter of the school year, I often flip-flop the roles. I often assign the role of Data Assistant to someone who is strong in collecting and recording the data, and that person can assist the others in learning their jobs. This pushes the thinking of all the students involved. This pairing challenges those who are not yet proficient with collecting and recording data and it challenges the Data Assistant to explain his or her thinking; the Data Assistant is not allowed to do the other jobs for his or her classmates; he or she must use words to describe what to do.

Questions for Differentiation
- *What do you notice about the data?* (Use an open-ended question like this to spark discussion and give you a sense of where students are in their thinking.)
- *Why do you think that?* (Use a question like this in response to statements such as "It's getting colder"; you are asking students to talk about the data and cite evidence; you are asking them to "prove it.")
- *What was the temperature on October 10th?*
- *What days during this month were the warmest? The coldest? The most mild?*
- *What was the lowest temperature this month? The highest temperature?*
- *What has been the range of temperatures this month?* (Emphasize the strategies for figuring it out by asking *How do you know?*)
- *What days so far this year have been warmer than today?*
- *How many days so far this year have been warmer than today?* (Again, emphasize the strategies for figuring this out by asking, *How do you know?* Some students might count one by one, some might group and skip-count, some might use the number of days in school and subtract, and so on.)
- *What do you think the graph will look like next month?*

Summarizing the Data Each Month with Mode, Average, and Range
- *What is the most common temperature this month?* (Mode)
- *What is the mean temperature for March?* (This arithmetic average/mean question would be appropriate for some third-grade students and many fourth-grade students.)
- *What was the range of temperatures this month?* (This question asks about the difference between the highest and lowest temperatures.)

In contrast to weekly or monthly data talk in third grade, we talked about the data every day with kindergartners and first graders. It was important for these younger students to discuss weather and temperature together on a daily basis, because each day they worked to negotiate meaning for these terms. How often have you had two kindergartners argue over whether or not it is cloudy because there is only one cloud in the sky? Amy and I facilitated many discussions about the difference between hot and warm, cool and cold, warm and cool, as well as about how to record the information accurately (see Box 6.2 for our conversation about hot, warm, cool, and cold). These young students need daily practice. You might find that daily practice as a class is necessary in second grade for much of the year before individual students are responsible for recording the data. In my third-grade class, although students were doing the data collection jobs, we spent quite a bit of time during the first and second quarters discussing how the Weather Watcher read the thermometer and recorded the data on the line graph, how the Daytime Tracker knew where to draw the line for 7:04 a.m. as the stopping point for the bar on the double bar graph, and what 84 degrees Fahrenheit felt like. You know your students' needs and you can adjust the management part of data collection as well as the frequency of whole-class experiences to suit your class. The key here is consistency—the data need to be collected daily so that students really see and understand the trends and patterns over time.

COUNTING THE DAYS IN SCHOOL

Counting and keeping track of the days in school is an especially beneficial routine for kindergarten and first-grade students. This routine lends itself to talking about numbers, thinking about patterns, and seeing amounts. It provides an opportunity for these young students to count every day, see and experience an increasing amount, and think about numbers beyond 100. For second and third graders, there are a variety of reasons and ways to keep track of the days in school, from organizing a growing amount to developing sophisticated strategies for comparing two sets of numbers (days in school versus days on the calendar).

As a mathematics coach at Bailey's Elementary, I worked with a team of kindergarten teachers who described a problem they came across with keeping track of the days in school. They realized that students were getting very confused between how many days are in a month and how many days we had been in school during that month. "What are we counting?" became a common question. Teachers were not asking students to compare the days in a month versus the number of days students had been in school. The problem was that there were too many different numbers (day of the month *and* the number of days in school) for them to keep track of, especially early on in the year.

One of the kindergarten teachers and I decided to use this routine of Counting the Days in School at the end of the school day as a way to remedy the confusion. That way, the calendar routines, which students worked on during morning meeting or at the beginning of the math lesson, were separate from the Counting the Days in School routine. We used Counting the Days in School as a check-off system: "We are finishing the ninth day of school. Let's add 9 to our counting tape and move our circle on the number grid from 8 to 9. Wow, you've just finished up another day of kindergarten. You are nine days smarter!"

I have seen many different ways to keep track of the days of school. Many teachers use a place-value pocket chart, with each pocket labeled from left to right as Hundreds, Tens, and Ones. They add a straw to the Ones pocket for each day they are in school. Every tenth day of school, students bundle the straws into a ten and place the bundle in the Tens pocket on the chart.

Although this routine is effective in third-grade classrooms, it does not seem to be very effective for kindergarten and first grade. Students at this age are in the process of constructing early ideas of number sense and are not yet near understanding why you bundle straws every tenth day of school. This routine requires students to have an understanding of unitizing—counting ten straws as *one* bundle of straws or one ten. Students in kindergarten and first grade are grappling with early ideas of how we count objects and represent the count with symbols. Counting ten objects as "one" is difficult when you are still constructing the early ideas of counting, one-to-one correspondence, cardinality, and hierarchical inclusion. Understanding unitizing is a huge leap.

Many teachers believe that the straws routine for keeping track of the days in school is planting the seed for strong place-value understanding as students move into second and third grade. I used to believe that, too; however, I have seen time and again that these young kindergarten and first-grade students are more focused on what that quantity means and what it looks like. Using cubes instead of bundling straws seems to be an easier way for students to construct early ideas of unitizing and of the importance and efficiency of ten. Opportunities to see ten ones being connected to one ten (without the exchange that takes place with bundles of straws or base ten blocks) will help these younger students construct the ideas of "ten-ness." The idea of ten as a group is at the core of unitizing. Early on, though, many children are learning that 1 means one item. It is too confusing to bring in the idea that 1 can also mean one group of ten. That will come later. It is more important for very young children (kindergarten and first grade) to build visual images of the amounts rather than focus on unitizing.

Collecting items (like rocks or cubes) for each day of school and counting by ones seems to be a more authentic and age-appropriate task for students who are still figuring out what twenty looks like, how to count twenty efficiently, and how to represent that number. The place-value chart does not yet make sense. Let's shift the focus for these young learners and instead create routines that will help them see amounts, learn the counting sequence, construct a sense of quantities, and recognize patterns.

COUNTING THE DAYS IN SCHOOL WITH KINDERGARTEN AND FIRST-GRADE STUDENTS

Descriptions of the most effective Counting the Days in School routines I have seen used for kindergarten and first-grade students are elaborated in the following sections. These routines include the focus on seeing amounts to understand quantity, the counting sequence, cardinality, hierarchical inclusion, and noticing patterns. What seems to add to the power of these routines is that they are based on a variety of models, such as a linear model of numbers, a number grid, and manipulatives, including cubes (eventually sticks of ten) and a rock collection. Using these different models within one routine helps to make the routine rich enough for all learners to have access to it and be challenged by it.

A Linear Model for Counting the Days in School

Starting on the first day of school, you can begin the work of building a "counting tape," an idea borrowed from *Every Day Counts Calendar Math* (Kanter et al. 2005) that emphasizes each tenth day of school. Amy and I had a Kindergarten Counter (a classroom job title) write the number of the school day on a sticky note and stick it to a sentence strip. The sentence strip would eventually fit ten sticky notes (1 through 10). Days one through ten were each a different color sticky note. Then, we started that color pattern over again until we got to twenty, then again to thirty, and so on. This model helps students with the counting sequence and especially helps kindergarten students understand the idea that the numbers are increasing as they add one number at a time to the counting tape. The color pattern of the sticky notes emphasizes the patterns in the number sequence. For instance, every tenth day of school will be light purple and every number with a 1 in the ones place will be dark pink.

Note: A number line is an infinitely long line on which every point corresponds to a real number and every real number corresponds to a point. The model in this example is not a number line because we did not designate points for each number, nor did we represent the infinite length with arrows on each end (we actually used line segments). This is the reason I use the *Every Day Counts* term "counting tape." I believe this linear model prepares students to understand and use a number line.

An Array Model (the Number Grid) and Counting the Days in School

Many teachers use a number grid—or hundreds chart—to keep track of the number of days in school (see Figure 6.4). They post a number grid showing 0 to 180 (see Appendix B). Copy and enlarge this reproducible on a poster maker and have students move a circle (we used Wikki Stix) to the next number each day. The number grid model can be difficult for students new to counting. Remember that it is a skill for students to move from 20 down to the next row beginning with 21. This is called a return sweep in reading, which is the horizontal-diagonal eye movement that is used when guiding the eyes from the end of one line of text to the beginning of another. Also,

Figure 6.4
**Eva keeps track of the days in
school on the number grid.**

students using the number grid see the numbers 0 to 180 all at one time, as opposed to what they see with the counting tape model, where they add one number at a time in one long line. Although it is often a more difficult model for kindergartners, students tend to notice different patterns on the number grid model because they can see the numbers 0 to 180 all at the same time.

There are some arguments over the appropriateness of the number grid model for kindergarten and first-grade students, because there are concerns that young students may just see a maze of numbers. Some argue that it should be built much like the counting tape. Nevertheless, I believe that it is important to have a model where students see a small number, like 5, in relation to larger numbers. In addition, I have seen many kindergarten students use the number grid model and a sophisticated counting up strategy to count the days until the much anticipated 100th Day of School Celebration.

Emma, a kindergartner, was especially excited for the 100th Day of School Celebration, and around day 75 she started counting the number of school days left until the 100th day of school on a number grid. On the 92nd day of school, Emma counted the number of days left until the 100th day and cheerfully stated, "Eight days until the 100 celebration!" However, instead of counting at the end of the day, as she had done on previous days , this time she counted first thing in the morning. Marcos was watching her do this and said, "You have to count today, too, because we're not done with today . . . we're not 92 days smarter yet." Emma was counting from the 92nd day, whereas Marcos was counting from the 91st day, because the 92nd day was not complete. Both students were using a sophisticated counting up strategy, aided by the number grid, and engaged in an excellent debate considering whether or not to start counting up from 91 or 92.

Manipulatives and Counting the Days in School

Counting cubes and, eventually, organizing them into tens sticks to keep track of the number of days in school provides a strong concrete and visual model for young mathematicians (see Figure 6.5). In Amy's classroom, the Kindergarten Counter added a cube to our Counting to 100 bucket each day. The idea is that eventually the kindergartners will start to organize these cubes into sticks of ten as they play with and construct the beginning understandings of unitizing. Give it time and it will happen.

First, our students decided that the cubes should be snapped together in one long line. They loved lining up all the cubes in one long line and

Figure 6.5
Students use cubes to keep track of the number of days in school.

"seeing" that number! Later, students tried to decide what to do with the cubes when the stick was getting too long and breaking. Our students did not organize them into tens right away. They broke them into shorter sticks, but they were not in tens.

Eventually, Amy and I prompted them to try tens; however, we encouraged tens too early. Consequently, many of them had no idea why we were organizing the cubes in tens. They were doing what we prompted, but the understanding wasn't there. We recommend waiting it out until a student eventually comes up with the idea (they will come up with other ideas, too, like fives or fourteens—let them play around with some of these ideas and ask, *Which works best?*). Keep in mind that it's okay for this to occur when it is March of kindergarten or December of first grade—we found that it is better for students to construct the idea themselves a bit later in the year rather than impose it on them too early. The opportunity to construct the understanding of unitizing and utilizing the "friendly ten" comes about easily (although with patience and much waiting) with the cubes. The cubes are eventually difficult to manage when they are in one long stick and take too long to count when they are not connected. This is a perfect scenario for your class to problem solve and figure out how to best organize this system for keeping track of the days in school. It becomes a real situation in which students can apply number sense ideas and problem solve.

Although Amy and I imposed *our* idea of organizing the cubes into tens too early, by March they were enjoying counting by tens, then ones: 10, 20, 30, 40, 50, 60, 70, 80, 90, 91, 92, 93, 94, 95. Counting the cubes by tens and ones every day helped many students with their counting sequence by tens and provided practice with the tricky skill of counting by tens when you have sticks of ten connected cubes, but then counting on by ones when you have single cubes. The children also loved seeing what the cubes looked like in one long stick on the floor. The Kindergarten Counter would attach all the sticks of ten cubes together to form one long stick as he or she counted, then systematically break them back into tens and place them back in their jar. The physical actions of attaching all the sticks of ten into one long line then decomposing that amount back into tens helped students see that numbers can be composed and decomposed. Furthermore, forming one long stick and then breaking it into tens helped our students continue to think about and see this magical number ten, planting the seed for a solid understanding of "ten-ness" and place value in a way that was authentic (counting and keeping track of each day of school).

In addition to adding a cube for each day of school (which eventually emphasizes our power of ten system), we also had students add one rock to a large, clear jar for each day we were in school. This gave us a visual for that day's amount, and we watched it grow and get heavier. Experiencing what 52 or 100 or 102 looks like—seeing these physical amounts on a daily basis—helped students further their sense of specified quantities.

COUNTING THE DAYS IN SCHOOL WITH SECOND-GRADE AND THIRD-GRADE STUDENTS

So what does the Counting the Days in School routine look like in second and third grade? Some of the routines presented for kindergarten and first grade, or at least elements of them, might work well with your class of second or third graders.

To ratchet up the math or change the focus for older students, check out the ideas and examples in Box 6.4. You know your students best, so you should determine which routines will be most effective for your class (and every year is different, isn't it?). You may want to focus on the Calendar and Collecting Long-Term Data routines with your third-grade class instead of

---

BOX 6.4 ## Ideas and Questions for the Counting the Days in School Routine

Using a variety of models (a linear model, an array model, and manipulatives) is one way to naturally differentiate the Counting the Days in School routine. The following list offers other suggestions for differentiating the routine. This routine is used mostly in kindergarten and first grade. Nevertheless, second- and third-grade teachers may find it a useful routine for a specific class, particularly using the array model (the number grid).

Linear Model: The Counting Tape
Differentiate Through Questioning
- *What number comes next? How do you know?*
- *What will the next yellow number be? How do you know?*
- *What do you notice about our counting tape?* (Students might notice the color pattern, that every number with a 9 in the ones place is yellow, that after every tenth number the pattern of ones starts again, and so on.)

Array Model: The Number Grid or Hundreds Chart
Differentiate Through Questioning
- *What number comes next? How do you know?*
- *Let's count by ones to today's number. Does it feel like you've been in school that many days? Does it feel like a short time or a long time?*
- *What number will we move the circle to on Friday? How do you know?*
- *About what number will we land on in twenty-seven days?* (Notice the word *about* is used to emphasize an estimate.)
- *How many days of school until the 100th day of school?*
- *What patterns are you seeing?* (The number grid is plentiful with patterns, and you can discuss this question throughout the year and at all grade levels.)

For older students (third- and fourth-grade students), encourage use of the calendar in conjunction with the days in school: Ask: *What day will it be on the forty-fifth day of school? How do you know?* Students will need to consider weekends and days you are not in school and will need to keep track of the days of the month and the days of school simultaneously.

Manipulatives (in our case, cubes and rocks)
Differentiate Through Questioning
- *How did she keep track of the cubes* (or rocks) *while she was counting?*
- *Why are we getting confused as we count all these cubes?* (Bring out strategies for keeping track of your counting.)
- *What is the easiest* (or most efficient) *way to keep track of counting the cubes? The rocks?*
- *About how much of the rock jar do you think will be filled up on the seventy-fifth day of school? Why do you think that? Does anyone agree, disagree, or want to add on to this idea?*

spending a lot of time with Counting the Days in School routines. Other teachers may realize that the Counting the Days in School routines are essential and may need ways to differentiate these routines. I hope that the ideas in Box 6.4 and other resources mentioned within this book will help you make these important instructional decisions.

TIME FOR REFLECTION: BUILDING ON WHAT YOU ARE ALREADY DOING DURING CALENDAR TIME

Calendar and data routines are fabulous opportunities for students to use numbers every day. They provide time for students to develop understandings about how numbers organize our lives, represent various types of amounts (such as days of school versus days in a month, temperatures, and time), and help us keep track of amounts. Calendar and data routines provide a forum for students to apply their number sense understandings every day.

Just about every set of curriculum materials contains ideas for calendar and data routines. The challenge for us as teachers is to figure out how to use the ideas to fit the needs of the students in our classroom as well as make the activities as authentic as possible. Some of the resources I use come from my district's adopted curriculum materials, such as *Everyday Mathematics*, 3rd Edition (University of Chicago School Mathematics Project 2007); *Investigations in Number, Data, and Space*, 2nd Edition (TERC 2008); and *Every Day Counts Calendar Math, K–5* (Kanter et al. 2005). Many of the ideas in this chapter are adapted from these resources as well as from the many wonderful ideas from the teachers at Bailey's Elementary. The teachers and I looked at what they were already doing during calendar time, how we could deepen the mathematics discussions around calendar and data routines, and what models and routines would most benefit students' number sense development.

Take time to step back and reflect on your current calendar and data routines and what your students are learning from them. What kinds of questions can you ask to ratchet up the mathematics discussions? Which models will help you better differentiate your routines? What are some ways you can better organize long-term data collection? How can you organize the data to best provide students with opportunities to apply their number sense understandings to analyzing data? There are endless possibilities in calendar and data routines!

A good routine, along with the questions you ask, will give you the opportunity to get inside students' heads and be aware of their thinking, understandings, and misconceptions. Because calendar and data routines occur frequently (most of them daily), it is an opportunity for you to watch students' number sense growth over time and how they are applying number sense skills and concepts within an authentic context.

PART III

MORE THAN JUST THE ROUTINE

7

LEARNING FROM EACH OTHER

Building a Strong Community of Learners Through Math Talk, Mistakes, and Reflections

Adam got stuck, but we waited for him, and he figured it out. After we counted, Lisa said a little bit about the pattern, I said a little bit, and we all shared our thinking and learned from each other.

This was nine-year-old Erick's response to my question, "How did we do with our Count Around the Circle routine today?" He noted that we gave Adam "think time" during the routine, then we held a discussion after the routine to talk about what we noticed about the numbers. Erick was recognizing that we become better mathematicians when we share our thinking with one another.

Building a strong and supportive community of learners is essential in making number sense routines beneficial and productive for everyone. A strong and supportive community is one in which children can share their thinking, talk out ideas that are not fully formed, work through their misunderstandings in front of peers, have time to think for themselves, reflect on their successes and challenges, and be supported on their individual learning paths to number sense. In *Making Sense*, James Hiebert et al. (1997) explains what it means to be a community of learners and why it is important:

> *Learning to be a member of a mathematical community means taking ownership of the goals and accepting the norms of social interaction. Why is it important that classrooms become mathematical communities and that all students participate? Because such communities provide rich environments for developing deep understandings of mathematics.* (43)

In order to build a strong mathematical community, I believe three essential components must be in place: math talk, using mistakes as learning opportunities, and reflections.

MATH TALK

The way human beings learn has nothing to do with being kept quiet.

—Ralph Peterson (1992)

Discussion among students is an absolutely critical component in their mathematics development. When students talk about mathematical concepts and strategies, they are using and creating knowledge. This occurs via two pathways.

One pathway is through the students' own talk. When a child participates in a discussion, she has an opportunity to "talk out," or voice her thinking. The process of verbalizing her thoughts brings further clarity to her ideas. The exchange of ideas that takes place in that process further builds her schema, constructing new ideas.

Another pathway for using and creating knowledge is through listening to other people's ideas. When a student engages with other children's ideas, he learns new ways of thinking, constructing meaning, and enriching his own understanding.

Talking About Visual Quantities

My third-grade students were visualizing one of the Quick Images dot cards I had flashed before them:

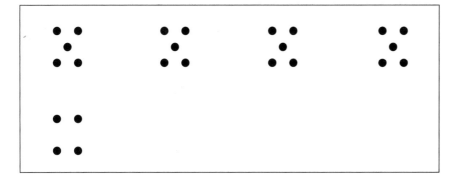

Jacqueline had that "I'm thinking really hard" look on her face, and then she smiled, showed a thumbs-up, and sat quietly. "Jacqueline, how did you figure it out?" I asked. Rather than ask for her *answer*, I asked her to describe the *process* for arriving at an answer.

Still smiling confidently, Jacqueline explained, "I saw four groups of five, then I saw the four so I counted by fives and that made twenty, then I just added on the four to make twenty-four."

I showed the children the dot card image again so they could see how Jacqueline had seen the amounts in her head. Yasmin responded, "Oh, yeah, I guess mine is kind of like Jacqueline's because I counted by fives, too. I counted five, ten, fifteen, twenty, twenty-five, but since the last group only had four and not five, I just took one out of twenty-five."

I jumped in to see if other students were understanding the girls' thinking. "Who is following their thinking?" I asked. I saw several thumbs-up, a few thumbs-sideways (indicating uncertainty), and a couple of thumbs-down (indicating lack of understanding). I called on Marcos, who had his thumb sideways. "Marcos, what did you understand about their thinking so far?"

"They both counted by fives," he replied.

"Can I add on to that?" Adib asked excitedly. "I agree with Marcos that they counted by fives, but Jacqueline counted by fives four times and Yasmin counted five times." As Adib restated their thinking, I wrote 5×4 and 5×5 on the board. "Yeah," Adib went on, "so she counted twenty and Yasmin counted twenty-five." I continued to write on the board as Adib continued to explain: $5 \times 4 = 20$ and $5 \times 5 = 25$. "Jacqueline added four to twenty and Yasmin took out one." I represented what Adib said with words and symbols below the equations by writing *then add 4* and *then subtract 1*.

"I see it now," Marcos said.

Anthony chimed in, "I saw it like Yasmin because I counted all fives, then took one out because the last group had four, not five."

"How many of you saw it like Yasmin and Anthony? . . . How many saw it like Jacqueline? . . . Did anyone see it a different way?" I inquired, waiting after each question for students to raise their hands.

"I saw it like Jacqueline, but I just thought of another way you could do it really fast," said Michelle. "You could think of two groups of five as a ten. So, see? It's two tens and a four, which makes twenty-four."

"Oh, that's cool," remarked Wesley. "That's easier with tens."

"You can write that one as ten times two and then add four," suggested Jacqueline. I followed Jacqueline's suggestion and wrote *(10 × 2) + 4* on the board.

I made a mental note of who participated in this discussion to ensure I got others involved in the next dot card discussion. "Get ready for the next Quick Image," I said. "The one we just discussed will help you with this one." All eyes were ready for the next dot card to be flashed.

This brief discussion gave several students an opportunity to talk out their ideas while allowing the rest of the students to see how others approached the visual quantity problem. In addition, the discussion highlighted a variety of strategies and reasoning processes that individuals might not have thought up on their own. The classroom community supported one another to develop their own ideas, hear different ways of approaching a solution, and make connections among concepts and strategies.

Each discussion looks different, depending on the routines, the numbers involved, the concepts that are highlighted, and students' varying levels of background knowledge and understanding. In all cases, rich, structured math discussions lead to deeper understanding and facilitate mathematical development. To develop a community in which mathematical discourse is central, focus on developing these four skills with your students:

1.   How to explain your thinking
2.   How to be an active listener
3.   How to have a conversation
4.   How to be supportive of your fellow mathematicians

You can build these four skills sequentially, although they can all be taught as integrated skills at the same time. Some groups of students may need more support in being successful in one area than in others.

How to Explain Your Thinking

Simply saying, "How did you get that answer?" or "Prove it to us" will prompt students to explain their thinking processes and illuminate their understandings. If students are not used to explaining their thinking, they may not know how to put their ideas, understandings, and strategies into words. You might get blank stares that say, "You want me to do what?" or responses such as "My brain told me" or "My mom taught me." That's okay! You just need to teach students how to explain what happened in their heads. You need to teach them how to make the implicit thinking explicit.

When students do not know where to start with explaining their thinking, scaffold their talk with questions such as these:

- *What did you look at first?* or *What part of the problem did you think about first?*
- *What number did your brain think of next?*
- *How did you* (or "your brain," if they keep telling you their brains told them) *know what to do after that?*

Questions like these will help students learn to look back at their thinking process in steps. Let's see what this looks like in the preceding Quick Images example from my third-grade classroom. If students had struggled with explaining their thinking I could have had them look at what they noticed first. They might have responded with something like: "First I noticed the groups were in fives because I just see that amount." Then, I could have had the children notice what they did with that understanding: "I don't need to count it. I can count by fives quickly." Finally, I could have helped them notice when there was a change in their strategy: "The last group I knew was four because I saw the two and two. I added that onto the twenty."

If students continue to struggle with explaining their thought process to make the implicit explicit, you can kick-start the process by telling them what you saw or by providing words for what you think they did. For instance, you might say, "It looks like you counted by fives because I thought I saw your mouth whisper, 'Five, ten, fifteen, twenty,' and then you counted up by ones: 'twenty-one, twenty-two, twenty-three, twenty-four.' That's what I think I saw you do. Did I see it right?" When I use this approach, I find that I can tell right away if I observed the student correctly or not. Many children are pretty quick to tell me, "Yes, that's it," or "No, that's not what I did."

Oftentimes students need visuals to support their verbal explanation. I write numbers or draw pictures on the board as a student is explaining her thinking, all the while asking, "Did it look like this in your head?" Also, many of the children listening to the explanation need a visual to understand their peer's strategy. It can be really difficult to follow someone's verbal explanation of her thinking. Writing what the child says as she explains her strategy, or symbolizing it with numbers, pictures, or an equation, makes it easier for the other children to *see* the thinking. Check in with the child by saying, "I tried to write what you said—is this what you were thinking?"

When students are explaining their process verbally, listen actively with the intent of understanding. Interrupt when it's not clear: "I understand what you did here, but could you tell me again what you did over here?" Sometimes I have to write down what the child is saying in order to "see" the strategy myself. And sometimes I have to repeat it back to the child to see if I truly understand, then ask, "Is that what you did?" I can tell if I've got it or not by the look on the child's face. Listening carefully and fully understanding what children are doing will not only help you facilitate classroom discussions but also improve your instruction a great deal.

It is important to have students explain their thinking both when their answer is correct *and* when it is incorrect. When a student's answer is incorrect and the child explains his process, he often catches his mistake or you are able to see exactly where the error or misconception is taking place. Also, the child's explanation creates a situation in which "prove it" doesn't mean "You've got it right," nor does it mean "You've got it wrong." It simply means "Explain your thinking process." As students learn to explain their thinking and the strategies they use, they will learn that their thought process is valued more than solely the right answer. Children will recognize that you and their peers will ask them to explain their thinking whether the answer itself is right or wrong. Talking through the process either confirms their correct answer or helps them arrive at the right answer.

How to Be an Active Listener

In order for a math discussion to deepen students' understanding, they must listen to each other attentively. Teaching the students how to be active listeners will serve them throughout their lives and will strengthen their mathematical understandings. Active listening means that one is involved in listening to understand and working to make sense of the speaker's message. In the mathematics classroom, we listen with the goal of understanding and/or expanding a mathematical idea or strategy. One way to begin the process of becoming an active listener is to learn how to paraphrase or restate other people's ideas in order to fully understand and/or clarify the speaker's message.

At the beginning of every school year, we spend a lot of time paraphrasing one another's ideas throughout the day in all subject areas. I have students talk with partners on a topic, then restate what their partners told them. To illustrate, let's look at another Quick Images example. In this case, instead of discussing the image as a whole class, I told students that they would tell their partner what they saw on the dot card. "I'm going to show you a Quick Image and you will turn and talk with your partner. Each of you will explain how you saw the amount. Listen closely to what your partner is saying and see if you can understand how your partner saw the amount."

I flashed this card:

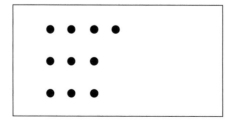

"Tell your partner what you saw on the dot card," I said. As the children talked, I listened in on their conversations. I took note of a pair who were listening well to one another and had different ways of seeing the card.

"Luis, you were really listening to Catie and trying to understand how she saw it. She saw it differently than you saw it. What did she tell you?"

Luis explained, "Catie pictured twelve dots because she knows six plus six is twelve. See, she added two dots there [pointing to the empty space] in her head, but she knew they weren't there so she did twelve minus two is ten."

To help Luis reflect on his successful active listening, I asked, "What did you do to understand?"

"I listened. She had to say it again because I didn't know where she got twelve the first time she told me."

"Yes," I observed, "I noticed that you asked her where she got twelve, then she reexplained and told you that there weren't really two dots in the empty space, but she imagined them there to help her solve it quickly." To relate Luis's experience to the rest of the students, I asked, "Did that happen to anyone else? Did you have to have your partner reexplain their thinking or say it in another way?"

We discussed what it means to be an active listener by using Luis and Catie as an example. Both reflecting on Luis's success with understanding what Catie explained and having him explain Catie's thinking rather than his own thinking modeled the skills of active listening. I then told students that we would practice our listening skills by explaining our partner's thinking rather than our own. We made a chart, listing things we could say if we didn't understand what our partner was saying, which included clarifying and probing questions and prompts:

- *Will you repeat that?*
- *I understand _____, but I don't understand _____.*
- *Where do you see the _____?* (In Luis's case, he asked "Where did you get twelve?")
- *Do you mean _____?*

I often noticed students referring to our chart to help them as they took on more active listening strategies. Eventually we took the chart down because this type of dialogue became part of our classroom culture.

To practice clarifying/probing questions and paraphrasing our partner's ideas, I have found that Quick Images work wonderfully well. Even if students do not see the correct total number of dots, they can talk about what they did see. A variety of ways of seeing the amounts comes out naturally with dot cards. Children become fascinated by all the different ways you can see an amount. It's a natural hook for listening to each other's thinking.

I find that, depending on students' ages and interpersonal dynamics, it can be difficult to get particular groups of students to listen to one another well. If this occurs, I work on listening skills in small groups of three or four, then help students transfer those skills into whole-group discussions around the number sense routines.

How to Have a Conversation

As students become more proficient with explaining their thinking and being active listeners, begin working on the norms for mathematics conversations. Start with a list of what good conversations look like. My students came up with this initial list:

- Let one person at a time talk while the rest listen.
- Face the speaker and use eye contact.
- Ask questions.
- Nod your head when you understand.
- Hold your thoughts until the other speaker is finished speaking.
- Disagree politely.
- Stay on the topic.
- Respond to the speaker with comments or questions.

Later, as we got better at holding conversations, we added the following to our "Good Conversations" list:

- Ask the speaker to "prove it" or ask him or her, "How does that work?"
- Learn from each other's ideas and mistakes.
- Make sure you talk, but also give others a chance to talk.
- Wait to raise your hand until the person speaking is done talking.
- Use "think time" and patience.

Your list should come from your students' experiences with conversations. As they get better at having good conversations, add those new successes to the list.

Teaching children to use language that helps them connect their ideas is a great way for students to have more fluid conversations. Connective language helps students stay on topic. It encourages a more structured and focused discussion. Rather than each person just throwing out his or her idea, you can teach students to connect their ideas and build on one another's thinking through connective language (Bomer and Bomer 2001). Post these sentence starters and practice with them until using connective language becomes more natural:

I agree with _____ because _____.
I disagree because _____.
I understand what you are saying, but I disagree because _____.
I think this part is true, but I don't think _____.
I want to add on to what _____ said. She said _____, and I think _____.
This is like what _____ said: _____.

Practice conversations with the whole group or in small groups, or have students practice with a partner. You may want to start with the sentence starters "I agree with _____ because _____" and "I disagree because _____." Then, build in the other sentence starters as students learn to listen to one another's ideas and build on one another's thinking.

How to Be Supportive of Your Fellow Mathematicians

In order for mathematical discussions to be productive for everyone, the children need to know how to support each other's different learning paths. Everyone has strengths and everyone has challenges. You will need to hold class discussions to teach these elements of a supportive environment:

> Everyone's learning trajectory is different.
> We focus on the process rather than only on the right answer.
> We prove it.
> We give think time.

One of the main reasons children do not want to participate in math discussions is because they do not want to be wrong. Children need to be supportive of each other so that everyone not only feels comfortable to participate but also feels comfortable to take risks and be wrong from time to time. Having class discussions about this will set the expectation that it's okay to be wrong sometimes. There needs to be a clear message that everyone in the classroom has strengths and challenges, and that as a class, we need to use each other's strengths and support each other's challenges. This message shows that we value the *thinking process* over the right answer. Instead of emphasizing who is right or wrong, emphasize the thinking that's taking place. As the facilitator in this environment, you can highlight times when students are being supportive of one another and when a child dives in and takes a risk.

Let's look at an example of such an environment. My fourth-grade students were sharing ideas about a true/false statement routine we were doing. (True/false routines are not described in this book; for more information, see Carpenter, Franke, and Levi 2003.) We had discussed whether or not each of the following equations was true:

$$25 \times 5 = 5 \times 25$$
$$30 \div 5 = 5 \div 30$$
$$7{,}555 + (5 + 5) = 5 + (5 + 7{,}555)$$
$$600 - 32 = 32 - 600$$

There was much discussion about the commutative properties of addition and multiplication. The addition and multiplication equations were true, because changing the order of the addends (or the factors) does not change the sum (or the product). However, division and subtraction are not commutative.

"I'm not convinced that 30 divided by 5 equals 5 divided by 30 is false. Why can't we just flip them?" Marjorie asked as she pointed to the right side of the equation. She didn't understand why we couldn't just transpose the 30 and the 5 on the right side of the equal sign.

"They're not like addition and multiplication," explained Anthony.

"Why not?" argued Marjorie. What she really wanted was for someone to prove it to her.

There was silence for about twenty seconds. Most of the class had agreed that this equation was false, proved their thinking, and were ready to move on to the next equation. They weren't sure why Marjorie didn't see why it was false and they weren't sure how to explain it.

Finally, Daniel spoke up. "You can't do 5 divided by 30."

"Well, you can, but you have to have, like, fractions and decimals," challenged Nisaa.

"Yeah, that's true," Daniel said. "So, I guess that still means that it's not equal. It would be way heavier on this side," he clarified as he pointed to the left side of the equation.

"So why can't you just switch the 5 and the 30 then?" Marjorie said to spell out her confusion even further.

Another long pause. "I'm not really sure either," Catie admitted.

"I think I know how to explain it, Marjorie," Erick said slowly, still thinking. "It's like 30 cookies divided by 5 people. The other side says 5 cookies divided by 30 people."

Daniel concurred. "Right, that's why it would be fractions. No one gets a whole cookie."

"Can you restate that idea, Marjorie?" I asked, checking in on what she was following.

Marjorie restated the idea, but still was not 100 percent sure. "Where are you all in your thinking now?" I asked. Looking around the room, I saw more thumbs sideways than I had before Marjorie stated her confusion. "Marjorie did a really great thing," I observed. "She was not totally convinced that the equation was false and asked questions about it. It got all of us thinking and made us prove it. You sparked quite a discussion, Marjorie! You all did something mathematicians do. You tried to explain your ideas in different ways to support her thinking. That's what mathematicians do—they ask questions, debate ideas, and try to prove their answers." I assured Marjorie and others, like Catie, that we'd do more true/false statements that week to keep the discussion going. "It's okay if it's not crystal clear right now," I told them.

Our discussion demonstrated the elements of a supportive environment. The students did not criticize or dismiss Marjorie for not understanding, because they knew that everyone's learning trajectory was different. They took it as a challenge to convince Marjorie that the equation was false. Marjorie recognized that she could use her peers' understandings to help her own understandings. In addition, the whole discussion emphasized students' thinking processes. Marjorie knew that the answer was false, but she didn't know why. She challenged her peers to help her understand *why* it was false by asking them to prove it. And finally, I gave students—and the students gave themselves—the think time they needed to figure out how to explain the correct answer to Marjorie.

Because it is so important, let's focus a bit more on think time, a key element to supporting fellow mathematicians. It is essential that students have time to think for themselves and that they are patient so others have time to think. Reinforcing this will take practice, patience, and positive reinforcement. To encourage think time for everyone, I find that subtle, nonverbal signals are useful. In our classroom, we use the silent thumbs-up signal during the problem-solving part of a routine (before a discussion). The silent thumbs-up signal gives students an opportunity to show the teacher they're ready to discuss their thinking while giving other students the quiet time they need to think it through. I like students to use the silent thumbs-up instead of raising their hands when they are trying to solve a problem, like a dot card amount, because it is less disruptive. You'll still have students who impulsively shout out the answer, but that means you need to review why you use a silent thumbs-up rather than raised hands or shouting out during this particular time. In my classroom, when we need to go back to review this procedure, we discuss that we don't want to step on anyone's thinking and that we'll have a better discussion if everyone has had time to think about the problem first. Later, after we have agreed to begin a discussion, we use raised hands to signal to the entire class who wants to participate in the discussion.

Before we start a discussion, we reflect on how think time helps our community. The reflection provides a venue for students to express the importance of giving everyone time to think on their own. When students know they will have time to think for themselves, they are more likely to participate in mathematics discussions.

Reflecting on how think time is helpful also encourages everyone to be respectful of it. One natural way to do this is during Count Around the Circle. Inevitably there are students who struggle with what comes next in a counting routine. As the teacher, you know if you need to jump in at that moment or if everyone should just sit quietly for thirty seconds while the child figures it out. When the child figures it out, keep the count going around the circle. After you make it all the way around, go back to the child who needed think time and say, "I noticed you got stuck on ____, then you figured it out. What did you do to figure it out?" Other times, try this: "You got stuck and we waited for you. You figured it out. What was helpful to you?" This may spur a discussion about the strategy as well as exemplify how helpful it was that "everyone gave me time to think." As the teacher, your noticings are also important and you can share what you observed with words like this: "I noticed you all gave each person time to think. That was helpful to everyone in our math community."

• • •

Math talk guides students to clarify their thought processes, test their thinking, and expand their ideas. Math talk allows a group to exchange perspectives and question each other's reasoning, thereby expanding their thinking on a concept. Math talk benefits the entire classroom of students as a whole and builds good habits of mind in each individual child. Lev Vygotsky (1978) explained, "By giving our students practice in talking with others, we give them frames for thinking on their own" (19).

MISTAKES ARE LEARNING OPPORTUNITIES

Mistakes and/or misunderstandings are wonderful opportunities for learning. When students feel supported by their peers on their various learning paths, they are more likely to participate. Not only are they more likely to participate, but they are likely to participate even when they are not completely sure about their strategy or answer. This willingness to participate is key to students' growth.

Students' reluctance to participate because they fear making mistakes is a common road block to working out their misunderstandings. Students' misconceptions in mathematics are likely to surface during class discussions. This is fantastic! When this happens, students will learn how to work out ideas that are not fully formed. They are more likely to try new ideas, even if they are not yet quite sure how those ideas work. They are more willing to take risks in their learning. And, they are more likely to get their misconceptions cleared up and have a deeper understanding of the concept.

Marjorie is a student who did not participate much at the beginning of the school year. She participated only when she was absolutely sure her answer was right. Through the course of the year, as we built a supportive community of learners, Marjorie gradually began to ask questions when she didn't understand something. Later, she began to explain her thought process, even if she wasn't totally sure her answer was right. Then, a turning point came mid-year. I called on Marjorie one day during a discussion about a pattern students were seeing and asked, "What part did you understand so far?" She was quite unsure about this problem, and her reluctance crept in—she didn't want to answer the question.

Then, Sadia said, "It's okay if you're not sure, Marjorie. Get us started and we'll add on to your idea." That type of support from her fellow classmate prompted Marjorie to readily participate in discussions, ask questions, and even share mistakes. Not long after Sadia showed her support for Marjorie, Marjorie raised her hand as we were going over homework one day and said, "I got this wrong. Can someone explain it to me? Because I thought it was right." A week later she made a connection to this mistake and said, "I know that's the tricky part, because I remember that from my mistake last time." Marjorie was hooked! She understood that mistakes were a vital part of the learning process. Her understandings increased the more she worked out these mistakes.

One way to emphasize that mistakes are opportunities for learning is by explicitly pointing out when children learn from a mistake. In my third-grade classroom, children were struggling with counting past the century marks in certain sequences, like counting by ones from 992 to 1,002 or from 1,092 to 1,102. Anthony got stuck on the latter jump frequently (i.e., after 1,099, he wanted to say 2,000) and brought up his confusions on several occasions during class discussions. One week, he got it! He recognized that a jump in the counting sequence had a 9 in the tens place and that this was the tricky spot. Anthony said, "I know this is the one I always mess up." We gave him think time and he figured out what came next. I pointed it out explicitly by saying, "Anthony did something really important! He did something mathematicians do—he remembered that last week he skipped the hundreds place when he was counting and it messed up the counting sequence, so when he got there this week, he slowed down to remember where his mistake was and see if he could do it accurately this time."

The phrases and questions teachers use can create a safe environment for making mistakes. Much of this language coaches students through mistakes, and it shows students how to coach each other. Here are some examples:

- This one was really hard for some of you. Where was it confusing? What helped you figure it out?
- Did anyone [name the mistake]? A lot of kids do that. Why do you think this is a common mistake? What's the tricky part here?
- You got stuck, but then figured it out. What did you do?
- I'm glad that this routine challenged you today. A lot of you made mistakes—that means you're learning.
- Tell us what you understand so far, and then we'll build on the idea from there.
- Andy isn't convinced that this is false. Does someone have a way to prove it?
- You all think that eighteen comes next, but Daniel and Yasmin think eight is next in this counting sequence. How do we know what comes next?
- At first you thought you saw twenty-seven, but now you think you saw twenty-nine. Why did you change your mind?
- Did any of you make a mistake when you figured this out? There's a tricky part in here; can you find it?

Our language is powerful and sets a tone in the classroom. The language we use can build the idea that mistakes are opportunities for learning and that learning is a process.

As students start to see what and how they can learn from their mistakes, they begin to talk about their mistakes openly and constructively. You'll see students connect with what someone else is saying with statements like, "Oh yeah, I made that mistake, too." I see students who know what to do in a particular problem help others with their mistakes by saying, "I used to do that, too, but let me show you how it works. I'll prove it to you." When students are comfortable talking about their mistakes, assessing is easier for me because I can see where my students' knowledge is fragile. I used to ask Marjorie a million questions to see what she understood and what she didn't understand. Now, she can tell me. In addition, she tells me if she understands some of it but is not "totally convinced" (one of her favorite lines).

REFLECTION BUILDS COMMUNITY AND FOSTERS LEARNING

My fourth-grade students had just finished a discussion about Count Around the Circle by threes starting at various numbers (0, 230, 240, 299). I said, "Take a minute to think about counting by threes and our discussion about it. Give me a thumbs-up when you're ready to talk about something you learned or noticed during Count Around the Circle."

After students had a few moments to think, I called on Catie. She said, "The even-odd pattern. Like, 233 is odd, 236 is even, 239 is odd . . . that was really cool. I didn't notice it until Iliass talked about it." In the days that followed, Catie continued to look at even-odd patterns in other counting sequences. The reflection that day helped bring it to the forefront of her mind and reminded her to look for those kinds of patterns again. Catie's reflection involved something she wanted to remember.

Anthony also reflected on a pattern he noticed, but his reflection involved a "wondering." He stated, "It seems like 12 comes up a lot. When we count by twos we get 12—2, 4, 6, 8, 10, 12. When we count by threes we get 12—3, 6, 9, 12. When we count by fours we get 12—4, 8, 12. What else gets 12?" Anthony was wondering why 12 came up so much. His reflection brought up the idea of multiples and how 12 is divisible.

Lizbeth shared a community success during our reflection. She got stuck at her number during Count Around the Circle and told the class that the think time helped her so she could figure it out. "Lizbeth, you were able to figure it out. What did you do?" I asked.

She reflected on what made her get stuck. "I was thinking about 270 and said 273, but that wasn't right. I asked Alex to say his number again and he said 269. I got mixed up there, so I counted it out—270, 271, 272." She used her fingers to show how she counted up. Lizbeth was often able to use jumps of three more automatically, but it seemed that the jump over the decade had confused her. Her reflection gave her a chance to think about the numbers and what slowed her down.

My students and I reflect throughout the day. Taking time to reflect on new learning, wonderings, questions, successes, and challenges is a wonderful way to build a strong community of learners as well as instill a reflective habit of mind. Reflection takes place at both the individual level (one's own learning and processes) and at the group or community level. Individual reflection provides time for students to evaluate what works well for them and what challenges them, decide on ways to improve their learning, and ruminate on new ideas, building their schemata. By reflecting as a community, children realize that there are times when they will need support from others and there are times when others need their support. Reflecting as a community helps us see how we can use our classmates' strengths to support and learn from one another. It helps us see that the community is here for us when we are challenged with something. That's really what a community is all about. When this type of environment is established, children are more likely to participate and try new things in mathematics.

In our classroom, we reflect at the end of each math workshop every day. We also often reflect after a routine. In both cases, the type of reflecting we do depends on what happened during the math workshop or during a routine. Some reflection time is spent on classroom management and community building—how we work together, what was helpful to our learning, our successes, what hindered our learning, our challenges, and individual reflections on effort and effective use of time. Much of our reflection time focuses on our learning—the mathematics, the strategies used and discussed, mistakes that were made, and ideas that we learned or that made sense. Both types of reflection—classroom management and learning—build a strong community of learners.

Individual and Group Reflections

- Reflect on individual participation and thoughts: *How did you do? What did you do well today* (or *this week*)*? What was challenging for you? What did you like about math* (or *the routine or the topic*) *today?*
- Reflect on teamwork: *How did we do? What were we successful with today? What was challenging for us?*
- Reflect on support for each other's learning: *What was helpful to your learning? Was there anything that was not helpful or that was distracting to your learning?*
- Reflect on the mathematics: *What did you learn about* (a big idea in math)*? What do you think about* (a big math idea or a new understanding that was highlighted)*? What was your "aha" moment today in math?*
- Reflect on the strategies: *Which strategies did you use today that were effective? Did you learn any new strategies today? Did you try a new strategy today? How did it go?*
- Reflect on conversations: *What did you learn from our discussion today? What are you still thinking about* (or *What are you not sure about*)*?*

- Reflect on mistakes: *What did you learn from that mistake? What helped you make sense of this problem?*

In addition to reflecting on both classroom management and learning, we reflect in different formats. Catie, Anthony, and Lizbeth were voicing their thoughts during a whole-class reflection. Sometimes we use a turn-and-talk format to reflect on what we learned from our routine. Once in a while, I set aside time after a routine for a private reflection without a share time—the children simply have the time to think, and they keep their thoughts to themselves. The latter reflection strategy (private reflection) empowers the child to self-monitor. It sends the message and sets the expectation that everyone is a reflective thinker whether or not we voice or share our reflection.

There are whole books on the power of language to encourage conversation and reflection. (Two of my favorites are Paula Denton's *The Power of Our Words* [2007] and Peter Johnston's *Choice Words* [2004].) Reflection is not only an important aspect of number sense routines but also a skill that will stay with children through their lives. It is an important habit of mind. When children stop and reflect on their thinking and their learning, their understandings grow and deepen, they make connections among ideas, and they discover how they learn best. All of this leads to self-empowerment. They become more motivated and take charge of their learning. They also become more active participants in the classroom community—like Marjorie!

．．．

Number sense routines are highly effective for all students when a strong community of learners is in place. Math talk, using mistakes as opportunities for learning, and reflection help your number sense routines run smoothly, encourage deep thinking and discussion about mathematics, and greatly enhance students' mathematical development. (Appendix C provides tips for using the ideas discussed in this chapter.) The icing on the cake is that all these components of a strong community also impact your students' attitudes about mathematics and teach them to persevere. Working in a positive classroom community develops students' confidence in problem solving and reasoning as well as in communicating and representing their mathematical ideas.

8

PLANNING RESPONSIVE NUMBER SENSE ROUTINES

I watched my second-grade student, Malaak, work on the following problem:

Diana went to the store to buy some gum.
She bought 8 packs of gum.
In each pack of gum there are five pieces of gum.
How many pieces of gum did Diana buy?

First, Malaak drew eight lines, which represented the eight packs of gum. I expected her to then count by fives eight times. Instead, Malaak drew one dot to represent each piece of gum and counted by ones. She drew the dots in groups of five (on the lines that represented the packs). After she drew each piece, she counted each one again, arrived at the answer, and wrote 40. Malaak's work is shown in Figure 8.1.

I said, "I see just what you did, Malaak, and you really worked carefully through the problem and organized your thinking. Now that you've solved it, do you think there's a quicker way to count all the pieces of gum?"

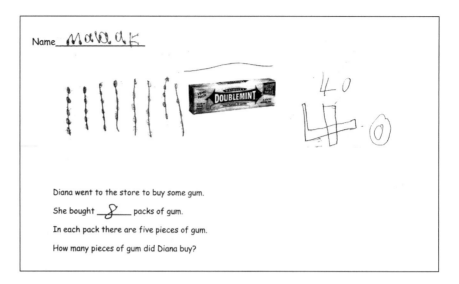

Figure 8.1
Malaak's Work Counting by Ones

Malaak looked at her organized drawing and said, "Umm, counting by fives would be fast."

"Oh, well try it and see if that works," I said.

"Five, ten . . ." Under her breath she counted, "Eleven, twelve, thirteen, fourteen," then said a little louder, "fifteen." She did the same to get to twenty, twenty-five, thirty, and forty. "Yeah, that works, too," she said with a confident smile.

As Malaak solved the problem, I prompted her to talk through her thinking aloud. Then, I asked her about a quicker way to count to find out if counting by fives occurred to her. Watching and listening to Malaak solve the problem, I learned a lot about her problem-solving strategies and number sense. I learned that she understood and could retell a multiplication story problem or situation, knew how to group quantities into fives, represented her thinking in an organized way, could count to forty, and could solve a multiplication problem accurately. There was a lot that Malaak was able to do in this problem.

I also learned that Malaak did not know how to count by fives fluently. I had seen her count by fives during a whole-group lesson, but when asked to count by fives within a problem-solving context, she did not do it fluently. She knew how to say each fifth number a little louder and with an emphasis (showing she knew what it meant to count by fives), but needed to count by ones to get to each fifth number after ten. That meant that counting by fives was not automatic for Malaak.

BEING RESPONSIVE TO STRENGTHS AND NEEDS: PLANNING NUMBER SENSE ROUTINES

Teachers use assessments, both formal and informal, to learn more about students' thinking and what they know and do not know. It is often difficult to figure out what students know, because it is common for teachers to focus too much on what students do *not* know. The intention is a positive one, as teachers seek ways to fill in the gaps in students' number sense and improve students' understanding. However, it is essential to have a sense of what students are able to do so we can build on their background knowledge en route to greater and deeper math understanding. Students construct learning based on prior learning; therefore, our instructional starting point should be what students know and can do.

During the interaction with Malaak, I was conducting a formative assessment. Formative assessments are ongoing, in-the-moment, dynamic processes that provide the teacher information during instruction. They are assessments *for* learning, because teachers use them to make instructional decisions and plan the next steps for students in their learning (Chappuis and Chappuis 2007/2008; Tomlinson 2007/2008). Based on the data I gathered from listening and watching Malaak solve the problem, asking her questions, and giving her time to explain her thinking, I was able to plan routines to help her implement a more efficient problem-solving strategy in the future.

I planned two weeks' worth of number sense routines that would help Malaak and others count more fluently by fives and apply that skill—and the understandings behind the skill—to problem-solving situations. I used Count Around the Circle, Choral Counting, ten-frames, and the rekenrek routines at the beginning of each of our lessons over a two-week period. The detailed plan for that time is provided in Appendix D.

After five days of the counting routines with the whole class and two days of counting in small groups, I pulled Malaak into another small group for guided math instruction and watched her solve another problem that encouraged the use of counting by fives. This time we worked on a measurement division problem:

> Somia, Kelsey, and Adam made 26 cookies for their friends. They put five cookies in each box. How many boxes did they need for all their cookies?

When Malaak worked through this problem, she drew a box and put five circles (to represent cookies) in the box, drew the next box and put five circles in the box, and did the same until she had four boxes. After she drew four boxes, she attempted to count by fives, and this time recorded the running total under each box (see Figure 8.2). She got confused at the third box (she wrote *12*, but immediately knew that wasn't correct) and started her count over again. She correctly said aloud, "Five, ten, fifteen, twenty." She knew there had to be another box, so she drew a fifth box with five more circles. She counted again from the beginning and said, "Five, ten, fifteen, twenty, twenty-five." Then, she added a sixth box and started to draw

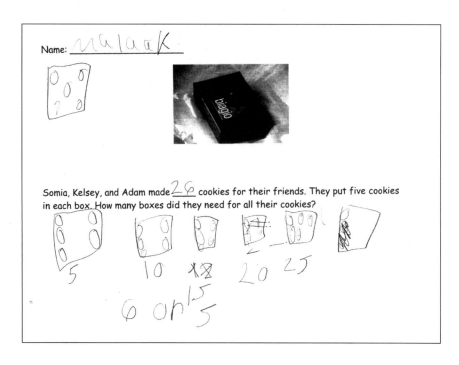

Figure 8.2
Malaak's Work Counting by Fives

another five circles, but stopped herself, counted from the beginning again and said, "Five, ten, fifteen, twenty, twenty-five, thirty." She realized that was more than twenty-six, then went back to the beginning and reverted to counting all of the cookie by ones. Although she went back to counting by ones (which helped her realize she only needed one cookie in the sixth box), I was able to see that she employed counting by fives, and I knew that we would need to work on counting that involved switching counting patterns.

While Malaak counted by fives in this problem, I observed that her counting was slow, but she wasn't counting by ones between each fifth number. In order to say the sequence correctly, she needed to start her count at five. I could see that she still needed repeated experiences with counting by fives and seeing amounts in groups of five, but she was further along in using a more efficient strategy than she had been the previous week. I knew it would be good for her to continue the experiences involving groups of fives and counting by fives, which I had planned for a two-week period. I would also plan some experiences for later that involved switching from counting by fives to counting by ones (for example, counting a pile of nickels and pennies).

HOW DO I PLAN RESPONSIVE ROUTINES?

Being responsive in this way can be challenging. You need to use your data from formative assessments with individual students, then think about the individuals as well as the class as a whole. You have to decide how to reach each student and how to plan experiences for the class. Not an easy task! This is exactly why teaching is a challenging and creative profession.

One of the many aspects of routines that I value is that they serve as daily, quick, formative assessments. They inform my instruction, helping me plan subsequent routines and lessons. Student work is another key component of assessment. I use my students' math journals, scratch paper, and tests to analyze their thinking and take a close look at their learning paths. I find that collaborating with colleagues to look closely at student work builds my ability to use student work as an assessment tool to its full potential. Let's take a look at how a group of my colleagues analyzed student work together.

Teachers Analyzing Student Work

As students get better at proving their answers by showing the process they used to get there, you can use their written work as a tool for planning. In our Math Collaborative study group with teachers, we used an analysis tool to help us get in the habit of looking at what a student was able to do and planning instruction based on the student's current understandings and skills. Mimi Granados and I developed a framework for analyzing students' work based on a Literacy Collaborative tool for reading instruction. In using our analysis tool, we first looked at the evidence and named only what was on the piece of paper. We were as objective as possible and only wrote observations. No inferences yet! For example, in the first sample of Malaak's work we observed that she drew eight lines with five dots on each line and wrote 40. Then, we analyzed the observations and discussed what the student was able to do and what he or she already knew. For example, because Malaak drew five dots on each line it appeared that she knew how to group quantities into fives and organize her work. We made inferences such as, "It looks like she knows to group the sticks of gum in fives." Also, because she wrote 40, we concluded that she knew how to count to forty. Then, we looked at what the student could almost do. This was his or her zone of proximal development (Vygotsky 1978). At this point, I shared with the group my observations of her behaviors while she solved the problem (instead of counting by fives, she counted by ones, then when prompted to count by fives, counted quietly between every fifth number). Based on the student work observations and teacher insight, we determined that she could almost count by fives and she realized that counting by fives was more efficient. Finally, based on the evidence, we planned the next instructional steps, including activities, routines, or other experiences, for the student. See page 140 for an example of the tool using Malaak's work on the gum problem. You will see the "Next Steps" for Malaak in the table.

See "Analyzing Students' Work, Thinking, and Learning" in Appendix D for more information about how to use the analysis tool in a way that can help you look at student work and/or help you talk with others (such as a study group, a coaching session, or your colleagues at a grade-level team meeting) about student work.

Analyzing Students' Work, Thinking, and Learning: Planning Next Steps for Malaak

Evidence of Student Thinking	What Can the Student Do?	What Can the Student Almost Do?	Next Steps
• Drew eight lines • Drew five dots on each of those lines • Wrote 40	• Groups quantities into fives • Organizes work • Can count to forty • Solved the multiplication problem accurately	• Count by fives: She counted five, ten, then had to count by ones but said every fifth number a little louder. Knows that five is a more efficient way to count the total	Provide experiences for her to hear others count by fives and experiences for her to count by fives. Use Count Around the Circle, Choral Counting, rekenrek, and ten frames.

Assessment and instruction are symbiotic. Assessment of the process by which students get an answer provides you with valuable information about their number sense. Getting students to explain their thinking process and analyzing student work helps you see what they know and what knowledge is still fragile. The formative assessments combined with analyzing students' work will provide you with necessary information to plan your number sense routines.

CONCLUSION
A Place to Begin

We play with numbers every day. That's why I get how to solve these problems.

—Kevin, seven years old

Sometimes we count by tens, sometimes we count backward, sometimes we count by really small numbers like one-sixteenth . . . all of it will help you solve your math problems.

—Sadia, nine years old

Numerical literacy is the goal. We want students to use their number sense to reason and solve problems. My hope is that you have gained ideas for number sense routines, received tools for planning and instruction, and learned effective strategies for facilitating your students' journey to numerical literacy. Visual quantities routines, counting routines, playing with quantities routines, and calendar routines all work together to provide multiple and varied number sense experiences for students. As children are actively involved in these routines daily and over time, they learn how numbers work, visualize amounts in their heads, see patterns in numbers, and understand relationships among numbers.

As you get started with number sense routines, I advise you to start small, build a strong community of learners, and get your students talking to each other about mathematics. This will lead to successful, meaningful number sense routines.

START SMALL

I have found that Quick Images routines are a good place to begin for several reasons. Quick Images routines will help you build a community around sharing different ideas and strategies. There are so many different ways to see an amount or put amounts together that this routine encourages students to value the fact that everyone's brain works differently. The dot cards and ten frames are easy to talk about and help children understand that they can get new, interesting ideas from their peers.

Some Ideas for Starting Out
- Use four to five dot cards every day for two to three weeks.
- Use teacher language like this to facilitate discussion:
  - *How did you see it?*
  - *Did you see it the same way Jennifer did or a different way?*
  - *Look at all the different ways we think about the same card!*

Then, try Count Around the Circle—this will help your students work on being a team, being patient with one another, and using wait time, and will help them practice active listening. Count Around the Circle provides a training ground for whole-class math discussions.

Some Ideas for Starting Out
- Start slowly. Start with counting by ones and tens.
- To initiate math talk about the counting sequences, simply ask, *What do you notice?*
- Practice think time if someone gets stuck. Discuss how helpful it was to allow the person to figure it out on his or her own and give him or her time to do it.
- Emphasize that mistakes are okay and important—value strategies and thinking (not just the right answer). Use prompts like this:
  - *When we were counting, you got stuck, then you figured it out. What did you do to figure it out?*

- Encourage reflection with questions like this:
  o *What was challenging for us today? What was successful?*
  o *What did we do to work like a team? To support each other?*

I believe that a strong community of learners in conjunction with an environment that encourages discussion about mathematics ideas is absolutely essential in making number sense routines successful. I'll reiterate some key ideas from Chapter 7 in a list format to help you get started.

Build a Community of Mathematicians
- Establish routines and rituals for your math workshop.
- Do your routines in the same place and at the same time each day.
- Discuss the importance of mistakes.
- Have conversations about what it looks like and sounds like to support each other as we are all learning.

Get Students Talking and Engage Everyone in Discourse
- Practice active listening with turn-and-talk, in small groups, with the whole class, and with questions and prompts like this:
  o *Say that again.*
  o *Do you mean . . . ?*
  o *Can you restate [paraphrase] what your partner just said?*
- Teach the use of connective language, such as the following:
  o *I agree with . . .*
  o *I want to add on to what _____ said . . .*
  o *I understand what you are saying, but I think . . .*

I wish you joy and success as you embark on number sense routines with your students. Developing one's number sense is never "done"; therefore, enjoy the voyage of the continuous development, and be in awe of the different paths children take on their individual journeys. It is a fascinating process!

APPENDIX A

Dot Cards

DOUBLES-PLUS-ONE AND MINUS-ONE SEQUENCES

1

2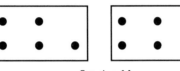

Two common ways to see this:

4 + 5 = 9	4 + 5 = 9
because	because
4 + 4 = 8	5 + 5 = 10
and there's one	and there's one
more	less

3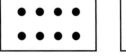

5 + 6 = 11
because 6 + 6 = 12
−1 ↓   ↓ −1
5 + 6 = 11

Some students might see groupings in fours and do
4 + 4 = 8.
There are still three more, so 8 + 3 = 11.
When children say this, I record it on the board like this:

4 + 4 = 8 ⟶ 8 + 3 = 11

1

Children often see 4 + 4 or count by twos.

2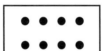

8 + 7 = 15
Children might use 8 + 8 = 16 and take one
off or 7 + 7 = 14 and put one back on.

3

8 + 9 = 17

This combination encourages children to use
8 + 8 to help them solve 8 + 9, but another great strategy
children use is to add one to the 9 to make 10.

8 + 9
+1 ↓
8 + 10 = 18
−1 ↓   ↓ −1
8 + 9 = 17

Number Sense Routines: Building Numerical Literacy Every Day in Grades K–3 by Jessica F. Shumway. Copyright © 2011. Stenhouse Publishers.

PLAYING WITH MULTIPLICATIVE IDEAS
(SKIP-COUNTING, GROUPINGS, MULTIPLES)

1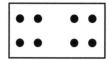

Students might see two groups of 4 or four groups of 2, although this arrangement highlights two groups of 4.

2

Many ideas and ways of thinking will come out of this card. A sample of some:

Four groups of 4	4 + 4 is 8 and 8 + 8 is 16 (double-double)	4 × 2 = 8 4 × 2 = 8 so 4 × 4 = 16

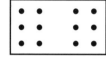

three groups of four
4, 8, 12
3 × 4 = 12

2

four groups of three
3, 6, 9, 12
4 × 3 = 12

two groups of six
6, 12
2 × 6 = 12

4, 8, 9
4 × 2 = 8 → plus one more is 9

2

3, 6, 9
3 × 3 = 9

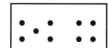

5 × 2 = 10 → minus one is 9
4 × 2 = 8 → plus one is 9

These are all ways to "see" nine.

Number Sense Routines: Building Numerical Literacy Every Day in Grades K–3 by Jessica F. Shumway. Copyright © 2011. Stenhouse Publishers.

PLAYING AROUND WITH THREE, FOUR, AND FIVE

DOT CARD SEQUENCES TO TRY

Number Sense Routines: Building Numerical Literacy Every Day in Grades K–3 by Jessica F. Shumway. Copyright © 2011. Stenhouse Publishers.

1

With initial dot card work, many students will be able to perceptually subitize and say "five" without counting one by one.

2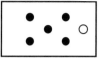

The unshaded dot highlights the idea of five and one more.

3

The combination highlights the idea that 5 + 6 = 11, because 5 + 5 = 10 and there's one extra on the second card.

5 + 5 = 10

+1 ↓   ↓ +1

5 + 6 = 11

4

The two unshaded dots highlight the idea of five and two more. Students conceptually subitize seven or count up from five (⑤ , 6, 7).

5 Show together.

Two common ways to see this:

6 + 7 = 13 because 6 + 6 = 12, so one more is 13	5 + 5 = 10 and there are 3 extras, so 6 + 7 = 13

Dot card sequences 1 through 5 may be all you want to do in one routine. Depending on your assessments of students' thinking you could try sequences 6 and 7 next time.

6

The 5 + 5 is highlighted to help students solve 7 + 8. If you show this combination right after the sequence 5 (the 6 + 7), some students might see that 6 + 7 can help them solve 7 + 8 and get into a discussion about the relationship between 7 + 8 and 6 + 7.

7 Review some of the cards from sequences 1–5, then show these:

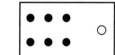 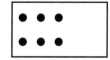

Students see the six arranged differently. The unshaded dot off to the side highlights 7 + 6 = 13, because

6 + 6 = 12

+1 ↓   ↓ +1

7 + 6 = 13

APPENDIX B

Counting Routines
Materials

TEN-FRAMES

Number Sense Routines: Building Numerical Literacy Every Day in Grades K–3 by Jessica F. Shumway. Copyright © 2011. Stenhouse Publishers.

DOT CARDS FOR TEEN NUMBERS

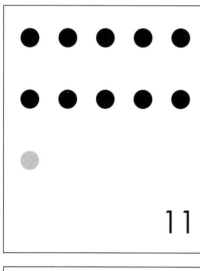

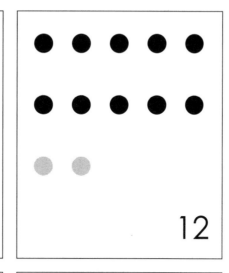

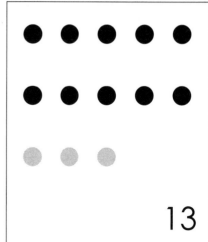

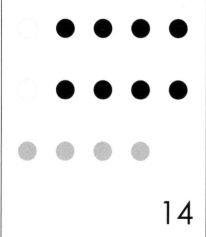

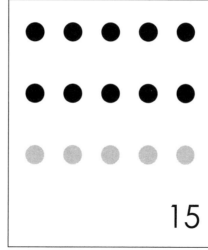

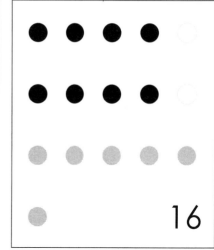

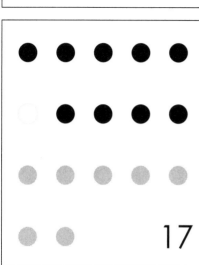

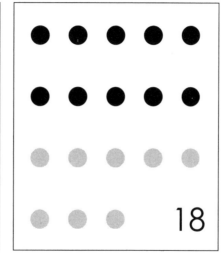

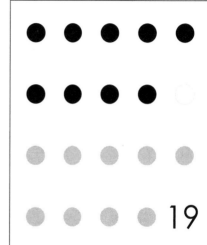

NUMBER GRID
0–30

									0
1	2	3	4	5	6	7	8	9	10
11	12	13	14	15	16	17	18	19	20
21	22	23	24	25	26	27	28	29	30

NUMBER GRID
0–50

									0
1	2	3	4	5	6	7	8	9	10
11	12	13	14	15	16	17	18	19	20
21	22	23	24	25	26	27	28	29	30
31	32	33	34	35	36	37	38	39	40
41	42	43	44	45	46	47	48	49	50

NUMBER GRID
0–110

									0
1	2	3	4	5	6	7	8	9	10
11	12	13	14	15	16	17	18	19	20
21	22	23	24	25	26	27	28	29	30
31	32	33	34	35	36	37	38	39	40
41	42	43	44	45	46	47	48	49	50
51	52	53	54	55	56	57	58	59	60
61	62	63	64	65	66	67	68	69	70
71	72	73	74	75	76	77	78	79	80
81	82	83	84	85	86	87	88	89	90
91	92	93	94	95	96	97	98	99	100
101	102	103	104	105	106	107	108	109	110

NUMBER GRID
0–180

									0
1	2	3	4	5	6	7	8	9	10
11	12	13	14	15	16	17	18	19	20
21	22	23	24	25	26	27	28	29	30
31	32	33	34	35	36	37	38	39	40
41	42	43	44	45	46	47	48	49	50
51	52	53	54	55	56	57	58	59	60
61	62	63	64	65	66	67	68	69	70
71	72	73	74	75	76	77	78	79	80
81	82	83	84	85	86	87	88	89	90
91	92	93	94	95	96	97	98	99	100
101	102	103	104	105	106	107	108	109	110
111	112	113	114	115	116	117	118	119	120
121	122	123	124	125	126	127	128	129	130
131	132	133	134	135	136	137	138	139	140
141	142	143	144	145	146	147	148	149	150
151	152	153	154	155	156	157	158	159	160
161	162	163	164	165	166	167	168	169	170
171	172	173	174	175	176	177	178	179	180

NUMBER GRID
0–280

									0
1	2	3	4	5	6	7	8	9	10
11	12	13	14	15	16	17	18	19	20
21	22	23	24	25	26	27	28	29	30
31	32	33	34	35	36	37	38	39	40
41	42	43	44	45	46	47	48	49	50
51	52	53	54	55	56	57	58	59	60
61	62	63	64	65	66	67	68	69	70
71	72	73	74	75	76	77	78	79	80
81	82	83	84	85	86	87	88	89	90
91	92	93	94	95	96	97	98	99	100
101	102	103	104	105	106	107	108	109	110
111	112	113	114	115	116	117	118	119	120
121	122	123	124	125	126	127	128	129	130
131	132	133	134	135	136	137	138	139	140
141	142	143	144	145	146	147	148	149	150
151	152	153	154	155	156	157	158	159	160
161	162	163	164	165	166	167	168	169	170
171	172	173	174	175	176	177	178	179	180
181	182	183	184	185	186	187	188	189	190
191	192	193	194	195	196	197	198	199	200
201	202	203	204	205	206	207	208	209	210
211	212	213	214	215	216	217	218	219	220
221	222	223	224	225	226	227	228	229	230
231	232	233	234	235	236	237	238	239	240
241	242	243	244	245	246	247	248	249	250
251	252	253	254	255	256	257	258	259	260
261	262	263	264	265	266	267	268	269	270
271	272	273	274	275	276	277	278	279	280

APPENDIX C

*Tips for Learning
from Each Other
(Math Talk, Mistakes,
and Reflections)*

TIPS FOR LEARNING FROM EACH OTHER (MATH TALK, MISTAKES, AND REFLECTIONS)

Math Talk Tips

Having classroom conversations takes skill on the part of the teacher and the students. Use this appendix section as a guide to help your mathematics conversations run smoothly and to support classroom discourse around important number sense concepts and strategies.

Explain Your Thinking

To help children learn how to explain their thinking, say, *How did you figure it out?* or *Prove it!*

If students struggle with explaining their thinking, scaffold them with these questions:

- *What did you look at first?* or *What part of the problem did you think about first?*
- *What number did your brain think of next?*
- *How did you* (or "your brain," if they keep telling you their brains told them) *know what to do after that?*

Be an Active Listener

Students need to know how to listen to one another in order to have conversations about mathematics. Students can use these questions and sentence starters to help them be active listeners:

- *Will you repeat that?*
- *I understand _____, but I don't understand _____.*
- *Where do you see the _____?* (In Luis's case, in Chapter 7, he asked, "Where did you get twelve?")
- *Do you mean _____?*

Have a Conversation

My students came up with the following list, which outlines important behaviors for having a conversation with classmates:

- Let one person at a time talk while the rest listen.
- Face the speaker and use eye contact.
- Ask questions.
- Nod your head when you understand.
- Hold your thoughts until the other speaker is finished speaking.
- Disagree politely.
- Stay on the topic.

Number Sense Routines: Building Numerical Literacy Every Day in Grades K–3 by Jessica F. Shumway. Copyright © 2011. Stenhouse Publishers.

Number Sense Routines: Building Numerical Literacy Every Day in Grades K–3 by Jessica F. Shumway. Copyright © 2011. Stenhouse Publishers.

- Ask the speaker to "prove it" or ask him or her, *How does that work?*
- Learn from each other's ideas and mistakes.
- Make sure you talk, but also give others a chance to talk.
- Wait to raise your hand until the person speaking is done talking.
- Use "think time" and patience.
- Respond to the speaker with comments or questions.

To help students have a conversation (not just throw out ideas), use Connective Language Sentence Starters (Bomer and Bomer 2001) like these:

- *I agree with _____ because _____.*
- *I disagree because _____.*
- *I understand what you are saying, but I disagree because _____.*
- *I think this part is true, but I don't think _____.*
- *I want to add on to what _____ said. She said _____, and I think _____.*
- *This is like what _____ said: _____.*

Benefits of Mistakes

Mistakes are essential to the learning process. However, in order to feel comfortable with making mistakes and learning from them in math class, students need to feel a part of a strong learning community—a community where mistakes are received and viewed as a natural part of learning.

In order to establish a strong community of learners, one in which students know they can learn from one another and risk mistakes, try these questions and statements:

- *This one was really hard for some of you. Where was it confusing? What helped you figure it out?*
- *Did anyone [name the mistake]? A lot of kids do that. Why do you think this is a common mistake? What's the tricky part here?*
- *You got stuck, but then figured it out. What did you do?*
- *I'm glad that this routine challenged you today. A lot of you made mistakes—that means you're learning.*
- *Tell us what you understand so far, and then we'll build on the idea from there.*
- *Andy isn't convinced that this is false. Does someone have a way to prove it?*
- *You all think that eighteen comes next, but Daniel and Yasmin think eight is next in this counting sequence. How do we know what comes next?*
- *At first you thought you saw twenty-seven, but now you think you saw twenty-nine. Why did you change your mind?*
- *Did any of you make a mistake when you figured this out? There's a tricky part in here; can you find it?*

Reflections on Mathematics Learning, Mathematics Routines, and Teamwork

Reflection is an absolutely essential part of number sense routines. Without reflection, students miss out on making connections, asking questions, and solidifying new learning. Reflection is also a critical part of building a strong community of learners. Try these reflection questions after your number sense routines or at the end of math workshop:

- Reflect on individual participation and thoughts:
  How did you do?
  What did you do well today (or this week)?
  What was challenging for you?
  What did you like about math (or the routine or the topic) today?
- Reflect on teamwork:
  How did we do?
  What were we successful with today?
  What was challenging for us?
- Reflect on support for each other's learning:
  What was helpful to your learning?
  Was there anything that was not helpful or that was distracting to your learning?
- Reflect on the mathematics:
  What did you learn about _____ (a big idea in math)?
  What do you think about _____ (a big math idea or a new understanding that was highlighted)?
  What was your "aha" moment today in math?
- Reflect on the strategies:
  Which strategies did you use today that were effective?
  Did you learn any new strategies today?
  Did you try a new strategy today? How did it go?
- Reflect on your conversations:
  What did you learn from our discussion today?
  What are you still thinking about (or What are you not sure about)?
- Reflect on mistakes:
  What did you learn from that mistake?
  What helped you make sense of this problem?

APPENDIX D

*Tips and Tools for
Planning Routines*

PLAN FOR TWO-WEEK SERIES OF ROUTINES BASED ON FORMATIVE ASSESSMENT: MALAAK

Week of May 12
Count Around the Circle (discussed in Chapter 4)
- Monday
  Whole-Class Routine: Count Around the Circle
  > Count around the circle by fives with a visual model. (The teacher writes the counting sequence as students count around the circle so they can use the pattern to help them know what comes next. Then, the teacher facilitates a discussion about patterns students see in the fives sequence.)
- Tuesday
  Whole-Class Routine: Count Around the Circle
  > Count around the circle by fives without the visual support; encourage students to see the pattern in their heads.
- Wednesday
  Whole-Class Routine: Count Around the Circle
  > Count around the circle by fives starting at 30 and stopping at 145; use the visual support if students need it.
  > Also do Count Around the Circle by twos (based on needs of other students in class).
- Thursday
  Whole-Class Routine: Count Around the Circle
  > Count around the circle by fives starting at 50 and stopping at 165.
  > Do another Count Around the Circle sequence based on the class's needs or based on what comes up in other discussions during Count Around the Circle this week.
- Friday
  Whole-Class Routine: Count Around the Circle
  > Count around the circle by fives starting at 5, but this time tell students that we will go around the circle twice and ask them to estimate the number that the last person will land on.

Choral Count (discussed in Chapter 4)
- Thursday and Friday
  Small-Group Routine: Have Malaak count by fives by herself or with others in her group when I meet with her small group of five students during math workshop. This will be the warm-up prior to the story problem.

Number Sense Routines: Building Numerical Literacy Every Day in Grades K–3 by Jessica F. Shumway. Copyright © 2011. Stenhouse Publishers.

Week of May 19

Ten-Frames and Rekenrek (discussed in Chapter 3)

The following routines are designed to help Malaak and others solidify a visual model of fives and how to use fives flexibly. The cards and numbers used for each routine have been planned, but I have many ten-frames with five dots and ten dots available in case I need to adjust the amounts.

- Monday

    Whole-Class Routine: Rekenrek

    > Show ten beads (five beads on top, five beads on bottom) and ask students, *How many beads are showing?* and *How many beads are missing?* Show ten beads (this time, represent ten in various ways, such as six beads on top and four beads on the bottom). Ask the same types of quantity identification and part-part-whole questions. Ask students, *How did you figure out how many?* if they do not readily explain their thinking. Continue with fifteen beads and nineteen beads. In all cases, highlight how the five-structure helped students figure how many.

- Tuesday

    Whole-Class Routine: Rekenrek and Ten-Frames

    > Ask students for ways to make fifteen on the rekenrek. Again, discuss how the five-structure helps them see how many total without needing to count each bead.

    > Show the group four ten-frames, each with five dots (can either be on one piece of paper or can be four separate cards hung on the whiteboard). Ask them to explain how they know how many dots total.

- Wednesday

    Whole-Class Routine: Ten-Frames

    > Show the group three full ten-frames and one ten-frame that is half full (five dots) and ask students, *How many dots are there?* (Make all four ten-frames on one piece of paper so they are shown at the same time, so that students count or conceptually subitize thirty-five.) Discuss ways students figured it out quickly.

    > Show the group five full ten-frames on one piece of paper (show all at the same time) and ask students, *How many dots are there?* Again, share strategies for figuring out the total amount.

- Thursday

    Whole-Class Routine: Ten-Frames

    > Show the group five full ten-frames and one ten-frame with six dots (on one piece of paper) and ask students, *How many dots now?* Discuss and practice counting by fives.

Show the students four full ten-frames and one ten-frame with
seven dots (on one piece of paper) and ask students, *How
many dots now?* Discuss and practice counting by fives.

- Friday

  Whole-Class Routine: Rekenrek and Ten-Frames

  Plan Friday's quantities with the rekenrek and ten-frames based on
  Monday through Thursday's formative assessments of the class.
  Possibly use dot cards with quantities grouped in fives as an
  additional model for Friday. Discuss strategies for figuring out
  the total quantities efficiently and make connections among
  the models.

Choral Count and Start and Stop Counting (discussed in Chapter 4)
Combined with Quick Images (discussed in Chapter 3)

- Monday, Wednesday, and Friday

  Small-Group Routine: Counting, Rekenrek, and Ten-Frames

  This week, have Malaak count by fives at various starting points
  and stopping points by herself or with others in her group
  when I meet with her small group of five students during math
  workshop (she might need a number grid as a visual support).
  Try counting by fives starting at 20 and stopping at 55; starting
  at 10 and stopping at 40; and starting at 35 and stopping at 80.
  This will be the warm-up prior to the story problem. Also,
  depending on her response to the rekenrek and ten-frames
  whole-class routines, repeat some of the same (or similar)
  routines in small group.

Number Sense Routines: Building Numerical Literacy Every Day in Grades K–3 by Jessica F. Shumway. Copyright © 2011. Stenhouse Publishers.

ANALYZING STUDENTS' WORK, THINKING, AND LEARNING
Analysis Tool

Evidence of Student Thinking	What Can the Student Do?	What Can the Student Almost Do?	Next Steps

Process for Using the Analysis Tool

Evidence of Student Thinking	What Can the Student Do?	What Can the Student Almost Do?	Next Steps
(If you are doing this in a study group, the teacher of this student is not discussing, only listening.) Be completely objective Describe only what is on the page Do not make inferences yet!	(If you are doing this in a study group, the teacher of this student is not discussing, only listening.) Infer: Now make some assumptions about the student's thinking based on the evidence What do you think the student did and why? What does the student understand? What are next steps for the student?	(If you are doing this in a study group, now the teacher gets to respond to the descriptions and analysis. The teacher may talk about the child, what happened in class that day, observations of the student as he or she solved the problem, and so on, but everyone should stay focused on the evidence.) Think about problems this student has solved in addition to the problem you are analyzing. Is the student close to making a leap to a new understanding? Is the student using this strategy or skill consistently?	(If you are doing this in a study group, the teacher continues to participate in the discussion.) Based on your analysis of the evidence presented, what does the student understand, and now how do we build on the student's current knowledge and level of understanding? Where is the student's knowledge fragile, and what will help the student fill in gaps of knowledge or remedy misconceptions? What are next steps for this student?

REFERENCES AND FURTHER READING

REFERENCES

Bomer, Randy, and Katherine Bomer. 2001. *For a Better World: Reading and Writing for Social Action*. Portsmouth, NH: Heinemann.

Burns, Marilyn. 2001. *Teaching Arithmetic: Lessons for Introducing Fractions, Grades 4–5*. Sausalito, CA: Math Solutions.

Carpenter, Thomas P., Elizabeth Fennema, Megan L. Franke, Linda Levi, and Susan B. Empson. 1999. *Children's Mathematics: Cognitively Guided Instruction*. Portsmouth, NH: Heinemann.

Carpenter, Thomas P., Megan Loef Franke, and Linda Levi. 2003. *Thinking Mathematically: Integrating Arithmetic and Algebra in Elementary School*. Portsmouth, NH: Heinemann.

Chappuis, Stephen, and Jan Chappuis. 2007/2008. "The Best Value in Formative Assessment." *Educational Leadership* 65(4): 14–18.

Clements, Douglas H. 1999. "Subitizing: What Is It? Why Teach It?" *Teaching Children Mathematics* 5(7): 401.

———. 2007. "The Building Blocks of Math." Presentation at the regional conference of the National Council of Teachers of Mathematics, Richmond, Virginia, October 11–12.

———. 2008. "Urban Setting." Presentation at the National Council of Teachers of Mathematics Annual Conference, Salt Lake City, Utah, April 12.

Clements, Douglas H., and Julie Sarama. 2009. *Learning and Teaching Early Math: The Learning Trajectories Approach.* New York: Routledge.

Denton, Paula. 2007. *The Power of Our Words: Teacher Language That Helps Children Learn.* Turner Falls, MA: Northeast Foundation for Children.

Eves, Howard W. 1988. *Return to Mathematical Circles: A Fifth Collection of Mathematical Stories and Anecdotes.* Boston: PWS-KENT.

Fosnot, Catherine T., and Maarten Dolk. 2001a. *Young Mathematicians at Work: Constructing Number Sense, Addition, and Subtraction.* Portsmouth, NH: Heinemann.

———. 2001b. *Young Mathematicians at Work: Constructing Multiplication and Division.* Portsmouth, NH: Heinemann.

———. 2002. *Young Mathematicians at Work: Constructing Fractions, Decimals, and Percents.* Portsmouth, NH: Heinemann.

Hiebert, James, Thomas P. Carpenter, Elizabeth Fennema, Karen C. Fuson, Diana Wearne, Hanlie Murray, Alwyn Olivier, and Piet Human. 1997. *Making Sense: Teaching and Learning Mathematics with Understanding.* Portsmouth, NH: Heinemann.

Johnston, Peter. 2004. *Choice Words: How Our Language Affects Children's Learning.* Portland, ME: Stenhouse.

Kanter, Patsy F., Janet Gillespie, and Beth Ardell, with Andy Clark. 2005. *Every Day Counts Calendar Math, K–5.* Wilmington, MA: Great Source.

Kriete, Roxann, and Lynn Bechtel. 2002. *The Morning Meeting Book.* Turners Falls, MA: Northeast Foundation for Children.

McIntosh, Alistair, Barbara Reys, and Robert Reys. 1997a. *Number SENSE: Simple Effective Number Sense Experiences Grades 1–2.* Upper Saddle River, NJ: Dale Seymour.

———. 1997b. *Number SENSE: Simple Effective Number Sense Experiences Grades 3–4.* Upper Saddle River, NJ: Dale Seymour.

National Research Council. 2001. *Adding It Up: Helping Children Learn Mathematics.* Washington, DC: National Academy Press.

Peterson, Ralph. 1992. *Life in a Crowded Place: Making a Learning Community.* Portsmouth, NH: Heinemann.

Resnick, Lauren B. 1990. "From Protoquanities to Number Sense." Paper presented at the Psychology of Mathematics Education conference, Oaxtepec, Mexico, July 15–20.

Sarama, Julie, and Douglas H. Clements. 2009. *Early Childhood Mathematics Education Research: Learning Trajectories for Young Children.* New York: Routledge.

Seeley, Cathy. 2005. "Do the Math in Your Head!" *NCTM News Bulletin*, December. Available online at http://www.nctm.org/about/content.aspx?id=928.

Tang, Greg. 2001. *The Grapes of Math.* New York: Scholastic.

———. 2003. *Math-terpieces.* New York: Scholastic.

TERC. 2008. *Investigations in Number, Data, and Space,* 2nd Edition. Cambridge, MA: Pearson Education, Inc.

Tomlinson, Carol Ann. 2007/2008. "Learning to Love Assessment." *Educational Leadership* 65(4): 8–13.

University of Chicago School Mathematics Project. 2007. *Everyday Mathematics,* 3rd Edition. Chicago: Wright Group.

U.S. Naval Observatory. "Complete Sun and Moon Data for One Day." http://www.usno.navy.mil/USNO/astronomical-applications/data-services/rs-one-day-us.

Van de Walle, John A. 2007. *Elementary and Middle School Mathematics: Teaching Developmentally*, 6th Edition. New York: Pearson Education.

Vygotsky, Lev Semenovich. 1978. *Mind in Society: The Development of Higher Psychological Processes*. Edited and translated by M. Cole, V. John-Steiner, S. Scribner, and E. Souberman. Cambridge, MA: Harvard University Press.

FURTHER READING

These are the mathematics teaching and learning resources I constantly turn to for ideas and to further my learning:

Barker, Lindsay. 2009. "Ten Is the Magic Number!" *Teaching Children Mathematics* 15(6): 337–45.

Burns, Marilyn. 2007. *About Teaching Mathematics: A K–8 Resource*. 3rd ed. Sausalito, CA: Math Solutions.

Carpenter, Thomas P., Megan L. Franke, and Linda Levi. 2003. *Thinking Mathematically: Integrating Arithmetic and Algebra in Elementary School*. Portsmouth, NH: Heinemann.

Chambers, Donald, ed. 2002. *Putting Research into Practice in the Elementary Grades*. Reston, VA: National Council of Teachers of Mathematics.

Chapin, Suzanne H., and Art Johnson. 2006. *Math Matters: Understanding the Math You Teach, Grades K–8*. Sausalito, CA: Math Solutions.

Charles, Randall I. 2005. "Big Ideas and Understandings as the Foundation for Elementary and Middle School Mathematics." *NCSM Journal* 8(1): 9–24.

Dacey, Linda Shulman, and Rebeka Eston. 1999. *Growing Mathematical Ideas in Kindergarten*. Sausalito, CA: Math Solutions.

Kamii, Constance. 2000. *Young Children Reinvent Arithmetic: Implications of Piaget's Theory*, 2nd Edition. New York: Teachers College Press.

Ma, Liping. 1999. *Knowing and Teaching Elementary Mathematics: Teachers' Understanding of Fundamental Mathematics in China and the United States*. Mahwah, NJ: Lawrence Erlbaum.

Piaget, Jean. 1965. *The Child's Conception of Number*. New York: Routledge.

Secada, Walter G., and Deborah A. Carey. 1990. *Teaching Mathematics with Understanding to Limited English Proficient Students*. Urban Diversity Series No. 101. New York: ERIC Clearinghouse on Urban Education, Institute on Urban and Minority Education.

Sullivan, Peter, and Pat Lilburn. 2002. *Good Questions for Math Teaching: Why Ask Them and What to Ask, K–6*. Sausalito, CA: Math Solutions.

West, Lucy, and Fritz C. Staub. 2003. *Content-Focused Coaching: Transforming Mathematics Lessons*. Portsmouth, NH: Heinemann.

In addition to the books listed in the references, I have found that these are excellent resources on classroom discourse and building a classroom community that encourages talk:

Chapin, Suzanne H., Catherine O'Connor, and Nancy Canavan Anderson. 2009. *Classroom Discussions: Using Math Talk to Help Students Learn, Grades K–6*. 2nd ed. Sausalito, CA: Math Solutions.

Fay, Kathleen, and Suzanne Whaley. 2004. *Becoming One Community: Reading and Writing with English Language Learners*. Portland, ME: Stenhouse.

Nichols, Maria. 2006. *Comprehension Through Conversation: The Power of Purposeful Talk in the Reading Workshop*. Portsmouth, NH: Heinemann.

Parker, Emelie, and Tess Pardini. 2006. *"The Words Came Down!": English Language Learners Read, Write, and Talk Across the Curriculum, K–2*. Portland, ME: Stenhouse.

I use these curriculum and standards resources (along with my state's and district's standards) to help me frame my objectives for teaching mathematics:

National Council of Teachers of Mathematics. 2000. *Principles and Standards for School Mathematics*. Reston, VA: National Council of Teachers of Mathematics.

————. 2006. *Curriculum Focal Points for Prekindergarten through Grade 8 Mathematics: A Quest for Coherence*. Reston, VA: National Council of Teachers of Mathematics.

National Governors Association and Council of Chief State School Officers. 2010. *Common Core State Standards Initiative*. http://www.corestandards.org.

The following instructional materials have a number sense focus:

Childs, Leigh, and Laura Choate. 1998. *Nimble with Numbers: Engaging Math Experiences to Enhance Number Sense and Promote Practice*. Parsippany, NJ: Dale Seymour.

Greenes, Carole, and Carol Findell. 1999. *Groundworks: Algebraic Thinking, Grade 3*. Chicago: McGraw-Hill Education.

Greenes, Carole, Carol Findell, Barbara Irvin, and Rika Spungin. 2006. *Groundworks: Reasoning with Numbers* (Grades 1–5 set). Chicago: McGraw-Hill Education.

McIntosh, Alistair, Barbara Reys, and Robert Reys. 1997a. *Number SENSE: Simple Effective Number Sense Experiences Grades 1–2*. Upper Saddle River, NJ: Dale Seymour.

————. 1997b. *Number SENSE: Simple Effective Number Sense Experiences Grades 3–4*. Upper Saddle River, NJ: Dale Seymour.

McIntosh, Alistair, Barbara Reys, Robert Reys, and Jack Hope. 1996. *Number SENSE: Simple Effective Number Sense Experiences Grades 4–6*. Upper Saddle River, NJ: Dale Seymour.

INDEX